ClojureScript: Up and Running

Stuart Sierra and Luke VanderHart

O'REILLY®

Beijing · Cambridge · Farnham · Köln · Sebastopol · Tokyo

ClojureScript: Up and Running

by Stuart Sierra and Luke VanderHart

Published by O'Reilly Media, Inc., 1005 Gravenstein Highway North, Sebastopol, CA 95472.

O'Reilly books may be purchased for educational, business, or sales promotional use. Online editions are also available for most titles (*http://my.safaribooksonline.com*). For more information, contact our corporate/institutional sales department: 800-998-9938 or *corporate@oreilly.com*.

Editor: Meghan Blanchette	**Proofreader:** Kara Ebrahim
Production Editor: Rachel Steely	**Cover Designer:** Karen Montgomery
	Interior Designer: David Futato
	Illustrator: Rebecca Demarest

Revision History for the First Edition:

2012-10-24   First release

See *http://oreilly.com/catalog/errata.csp?isbn=9781449327439* for release details.

ISBN: 978-1-449-32743-9

[LSI]

Table of Contents

Preface

Who Should Read This Book

This book is for software developers who want to learn how to get started using ClojureScript to build web browser applications. This book will not assume any prior knowledge of ClojureScript. We do assume that you have at least a basic working knowledge of the core JavaScript language. For the sections of this book that deal with ClojureScript in a web browser, we assume you are familiar with HTML, CSS, the DOM, and how they are manipulated in JavaScript.

While this book will not assume any prior knowledge of Clojure, it is not designed to be a comprehensive reference to the Clojure programming language. We will explain Clojure language concepts in ClojureScript as they become important, but we also recommend picking up a book on Clojure for a more thorough guide to the language. The authors of this book wrote *Practical Clojure* (Apress, 2010) and O'Reilly has released *Clojure Programming* (*http://oreil.ly/Clojure_Programming*) by our friends Chas Emerick, Brian Carper, and Christophe Grand.

How to Use This Book

This book is both a how-to guide for using ClojureScript and a tutorial on the language itself. We have arranged the chapters in what we felt was the best order for someone who is completely new to the language but wants to get started quickly. If you already know Clojure or ClojureScript and just want advice on development tools and workflow, focus on Chapters 2, 3, 7, 9, and 10. If you want to dive into the language right away, start with Chapters 4 through 6 before reading about the development process.

Chapter 1, Introduction: Why ClojureScript?

In this chapter, we lay out the motivation for ClojureScript: why it exists and what role it is designed to fill.

Chapter 2, Hello World

In this chapter, we work through a complete, albeit trivial, ClojureScript application. We introduce Leiningen, the lein-cljsbuild plug-in, and how to use ClojureScript in an HTML page. We save explanation for later chapters, but this chapter should be enough to get your first ClojureScript code "up and running."

Chapter 3, The Compilation Process

This chapter goes into the ClojureScript compiler in detail, explaining how it works, most of the configuration options it supports, and how it integrates with the Google Closure Compiler.

Chapters 4 through 6 cover the basics of the ClojureScript language itself. Although not a complete guide to every corner of the language, they cover most of the features that are required for everyday programming. Because ClojureScript and Clojure are so similar, we recommend books about Clojure to learn more about the language.

Chapter 4, ClojureScript Basics

This chapter introduces the essential syntax and control structures of the Clojure-Script language including functions, bindings, scope, and interoperation with JavaScript.

Chapter 5, Data and State

This chapter covers the primitive and composite data structures of ClojureScript, and shows how to work with them in programs. In particular, it explains Clojure-Script's approach to immutability and state management.

Chapter 6, Sequences

This chapter introduces Lazy Sequences, an important data structure in Clojure-Script that makes up a substantial portion of the standard library.

Chapter 7, Namespaces, Libraries, and Google Closure

This chapter covers namespaces as a feature of the ClojureScript language and also explains how files are organized in ClojureScript projects. We go into detail about how the Google Closure Compiler affects the use of libraries in ClojureScript projects, and provide a detailed flowchart for determining how best to use any particular library.

Chapter 8, Macros

This chapter introduces macros, an advanced language feature provided by ClojureScript.

Chapter 9, Development Process and Workflow

This chapter covers a variety of alternative methods for working with ClojureScript code apart from the workflow we have used elsewhere in the book. We demonstrate some tools packaged with ClojureScript itself, including command-line compilation scripts and the ClojureScript Browser REPL (bREPL).

Chapter 10, Integration with Clojure

This chapter briefly demonstrates what can be achieved by combining Clojure and ClojureScript in the same application.

Conventions Used in This Book

The following typographical conventions are used in this book:

Italic

Indicates new terms, URLs, email addresses, filenames, and file extensions.

`Constant width`

Used for program listings, as well as within paragraphs to refer to program elements such as variable or function names, databases, data types, environment variables, statements, and keywords.

`Constant width bold`

Shows commands or other text that should be typed literally by the user.

`Constant width italic`

Shows text that should be replaced with user-supplied values or by values determined by context.

This icon signifies a tip, suggestion, or general note.

This icon indicates a warning or caution.

Using Code Examples

This book is here to help you get your job done. In general, you may use the code in this book in your programs and documentation. You do not need to contact us for permission unless you're reproducing a significant portion of the code. For example, writing a program that uses several chunks of code from this book does not require permission.

Selling or distributing a CD-ROM of examples from O'Reilly books does require permission. Answering a question by citing this book and quoting example code does not require permission. Incorporating a significant amount of example code from this book into your product's documentation does require permission.

We appreciate, but do not require, attribution. An attribution usually includes the title, author, publisher, and ISBN. For example: "*ClojureScript: Up and Running* by Stuart Sierra and Luke VanderHart (O'Reilly). Copyright 2013 Stuart Sierra and Luke VanderHart, 978-1-449-32743-9."

If you feel your use of code examples falls outside fair use or the permission given above, feel free to contact us at *permissions@oreilly.com*.

Safari® Books Online

 Safari Books Online (*www.safaribooksonline.com*) is an on-demand digital library that delivers expert content in both book and video form from the world's leading authors in technology and business.

Technology professionals, software developers, web designers, and business and creative professionals use Safari Books Online as their primary resource for research, problem solving, learning, and certification training.

Safari Books Online offers a range of product mixes and pricing programs for organizations, government agencies, and individuals. Subscribers have access to thousands of books, training videos, and prepublication manuscripts in one fully searchable database from publishers like O'Reilly Media, Prentice Hall Professional, Addison-Wesley Professional, Microsoft Press, Sams, Que, Peachpit Press, Focal Press, Cisco Press, John Wiley & Sons, Syngress, Morgan Kaufmann, IBM Redbooks, Packt, Adobe Press, FT Press, Apress, Manning, New Riders, McGraw-Hill, Jones & Bartlett, Course Technology, and dozens more. For more information about Safari Books Online, please visit us online.

How to Contact Us

Please address comments and questions concerning this book to the publisher:

O'Reilly Media, Inc.
1005 Gravenstein Highway North
Sebastopol, CA 95472
800-998-9938 (in the United States or Canada)
707-829-0515 (international or local)
707-829-0104 (fax)

We have a web page for this book, where we list errata, examples, and any additional information. You can access this page at *http://oreil.ly/ClojureScript*.

To comment or ask technical questions about this book, send email to *bookquestions@oreilly.com*.

For more information about our books, courses, conferences, and news, see our website at *http://www.oreilly.com*.

Find us on Facebook: *http://facebook.com/oreilly*

Follow us on Twitter: *http://twitter.com/oreillymedia*

Watch us on YouTube: *http://www.youtube.com/oreillymedia*

Acknowledgments

We would like to thank everyone involved in the development of ClojureScript as an open-source project, especially its creator, Rich Hickey. Thanks also to our technical reviewers Brenton Ashworth, Michael Fogus, and David Nolen, and to all our readers who sent in notes and corrections on early drafts. Finally, a big thank you to Justin Gehtland and Stuart Halloway, founders of Relevance, Inc., for creating a unique workplace that gives us the freedom to explore new technologies and contribute to the open-source community.

CHAPTER 1

Introduction: Why ClojureScript?

This book aims to get you up and running with *ClojureScript*, a dialect of the Clojure programming language that compiles to JavaScript. To begin, this chapter will provide some motivation for why ClojureScript exists.

The Rise of Browser Applications

Web applications have come a long way from simple CGI scripts, but they have always been constrained by the stateless request-response model of HTTP. As the "pages" in a web application become more elaborate, the cost in time and bandwidth of reloading an entire page just to update a single piece of information becomes prohibitively high.

One of the first major uses of JavaScript on the web was to ameliorate the cost of small updates, but "web applications" remained primarily *server applications* for a long time, and for good reason. Deploying an application to a web server is much easier than distributing it to diverse client machines: the server is a controlled environment, with many more options for programming languages and frameworks. But by treating web browsers like dumb terminals, applications were severely limited by how quickly they could push updates to a client.

Recent years have witnessed the rise of what one might call *browser applications*. These applications typically still have server-side components, but a significant part of their logic runs client-side, in a web browser. The web browser acts like a virtual machine, executing JavaScript code to communicate with a server, render a graphical user interface, and make all the local decisions that do not require a server. The result is a more responsive, more fluid style of interaction for client applications. While the original World Wide Web of hyperlinked documents will likely remain for many years to come, it seems probable that web *server* applications will be largely supplanted by web browser applications.

The Rise of JavaScript

Browser applications were made possible by dramatic improvements in the JavaScript execution environments packaged with web browsers. High-performance JavaScript engines such as WebKit's SquirrelFish, Mozilla's TraceMonkey, and Google's V8 proved that JavaScript could be fast and launched the browser performance wars. JavaScript began to succeed as a general-purpose application platform where other in-browser execution environments had failed. It was a historical accident that no one could have predicted, least of all the early developers of JavaScript.

Although JavaScript has many flaws, it has a few strengths that allowed it to succeed:

1. It is a small language. Core JavaScript has a limited number of keywords, concepts, and built-in features. This makes it easy to embed in different environments.

2. It is flexible. Features missing from core JavaScript, such as namespaces or classes, can be added using the language itself.

3. JavaScript functions are first-class. Although JavaScript is not a "functional" programming language in the usual sense, the ability to create and compose functions as values grants it immense power.

4. *It's there.* Every web browser has had JavaScript built-in since the mid-1990s. Beyond that, the ease of embedding JavaScript in other applications has led to its inclusion in products as diverse as databases and television set-top boxes.

The Need for a Better Language

Despite JavaScript's overwhelming success, it still has many flaws (see Douglas Crockford's excellent book, *JavaScript: The Good Parts* (O'Reilly)). It was a product of unpredictable evolution, not a carefully thought-out design process. And the vast reach and diversity of JavaScript runtimes is both a blessing and a curse: it will be difficult to create a new and improved version of the language that can replace all of the "legacy" versions deployed around the world.

So JavaScript is here to stay, probably in its current form, for some time. Some have gone so far as to say that "JavaScript is the assembly language of the web" (see Scott Hanselman's article, "JavaScript is Assembly Language for the Web" (*http://bit.ly/OtWURd*)). So now we are beginning to see the rise of tools and languages that treat JavaScript as a compilation target, much like bytecode on a virtual machine or object code in a traditional compiler. For example, the Google Web Toolkit (*http://bit.ly/W0zaqU*) compiles a subset of the Java language to JavaScript. We even have entirely new languages, such as CoffeeScript (*http://coffeescript.org/*) and Dart (*http://www.dartlang.org/*), designed to target JavaScript compilation directly.

Any cross-language compiler has to make decisions about where to draw boundaries between the source language and the target language. CoffeeScript, for example, is deliberately designed to have semantics very close to those of JavaScript, adding only a cleaner syntax and protection from some of JavaScript's more egregious flaws. Google Web Toolkit, on the other hand, is designed to hide JavaScript from developers who want to work exclusively with the Java language.

Introducing ClojureScript

ClojureScript is a version of the Clojure programming language, which compiles to JavaScript. Its primary target is web browser applications, but it is also applicable to any environment where JavaScript is the only programmable technology available.

Clojure is a powerful, expressive, Lisp-like language developed for the Java Virtual Machine (there is also a community-maintained port of Clojure to the .NET Common Language Runtime (CLR)). ClojureScript is more than Clojure syntax layered on top of JavaScript: it supports the full semantics of the Clojure language, including immutable data structures, lazy sequences, first-class functions, and macros. Explaining how to use these features in ClojureScript will be the subject of this book.

Clojure was designed to have a symbiotic relationship with the JVM: it does not try to hide all the details of its host platform. In the same vein, ClojureScript does not try to hide all the details of JavaScript or the browser execution environment. ClojureScript uses the same native types as JavaScript, such as strings and numbers, and can call JavaScript functions directly without any special "wrapper" or "foreign-function" code. ClojureScript is also designed to work closely with best-of-breed JavaScript optimization tools such as the Google Closure Compiler. These relationships will be explored in Chapter 3.

In summary, ClojureScript provides developers with a language that is more powerful than JavaScript, which can reach all the same places JavaScript can, with fewer of JavaScript's shortcomings.

CHAPTER 2

Hello World

The next chapter will explain in detail how the ClojureScript compiler works, and its various options and their applications. But for now, you probably want to jump right in and get started.

Due to the relative youth of ClojureScript as a technology, there aren't any highly standardized ways of working or best practices yet. What conventions there are tend to change frequently, and the built-in tools that ClojureScript ships with are somewhat low-level and labor-intensive to use.

Therefore, in the spirit of the *Up and Running* title of this book, we will recommend *Leiningen* and *lein-cljsbuild* as tools for getting started, and these will be introduced in this chapter and used throughout the rest of the book. They are more mature than other tools currently available, are relatively easy to use, work on all three major platforms (Windows, Linux, and OS X), and are likely to be around for some time.

Instructions for installing ClojureScript from source and running its lower-level, more primitive tools will also be included in Chapter 9. However, for most users, Leiningen should prove more than sufficient for both learning and real-world production use.

Java Development Kit

Clojure, ClojureScript, and Leiningen all run on top of the Java Virtual Machine (JVM), which is provided by a Java Development Kit (JDK). Many operating systems come prepackaged with a JDK. For those that don't, you can download one for free here (*http://bit.ly/TEA7iC*). Get the latest version of the Java Standard Edition (SE) JDK available for your operating system. Clojure requires at least version 5.

There are other JDKs available but these are not as thoroughly tested with Clojure and ClojureScript, so we recommend the Oracle JDK as the easiest way to get started.

Leiningen

Leiningen is a build system for Clojure, named to highlight its opposition to the venerable but labor-intensive *Ant* build system for Java (see the short story *Leiningen Versus the Ants* by Carl Stephenson). It is the *de facto* standard for building Clojure projects in the Clojure community, and has a wide array of useful features.

It utilizes Maven (*http://maven.apache.org/*) for dependency resolution, and can seamlessly connect to any Maven repository to acquire dependencies. However, it features an original build system optimized for Clojure workflows, and can also compile Java source code. In addition, it exposes integration points for third-party plug-ins, enabling its use with a wide variety of other programming languages, including ClojureScript via the *lein-cljsbuild* plug-in discussed below.

This book describes Leiningen version 2, which is much more featureful than previous versions and is recommended for new projects at the time of writing. If you do need to use ClojureScript with existing versions of Leiningen, don't worry: *lein-cljsbuild* is fully compatible with Leiningen 1.7.0 and up. However, you'll need to read the legacy Leiningen documentation, as the examples included here use new configuration properties introduced in 2.0.0.

Don't worry if some things described in this chapter don't make sense, or if you don't understand some of the syntax or terms used. Everything covered here will be elaborated in much greater detail throughout the rest of the book.

Installing Leiningen on OS X and Linux

1. Download the latest version of the `lein` script from the Leiningen GitHub page (*https://github.com/technomancy/leiningen*), and save it to a location on your system's PATH (typically ~/bin or /usr/local/bin).
2. Set the script to be executable (e.g., `chmod +x ./lein`).
3. Run the script (e.g., `./lein`). Leiningen will automatically download everything it needs to function properly.

That's it! You're now ready to use Leiningen.

Git and GitHub

Git is a powerful source code management system that is extremely popular among open source developers and is used for most open source projects. If you're not already using it, you can install it and learn about how it works from its website (*http://git-scm.com/*).

You will probably also see frequent references to *GitHub*, a featureful and easy-to-use Git hosting service that is free for open source projects. ClojureScript itself is hosted on GitHub, as are practically all ClojureScript tools and libraries.

Installing Leiningen on Windows

1. Download the `lein.bat` file from the Leiningen GitHub page (*https://github.com/technomancy/leiningen*), and save it to your hard drive.
2. Install either `wget` (*http://gnuwin32.sourceforge.net/packages/wget.htm*) or `curl` (`http://curl.haxx.se/`). These are programs that the Leiningen batch script can use to automatically download the rest of its dependencies.
3. Run `lein.bat`, passing it the `self-install` argument (`.\lein.bat self-install`). Leiningen will download the rest of its dependencies and finish installing itself.

That's all! Leiningen is now installed on your Windows system.

Using lein-cljsbuild

Leiningen does not yet support building ClojureScript code on its own. Fortunately, thanks to its plug-in system, using the *lein-cljsbuild* plug-in for ClojureScript development is easy: just reference it in the `:plugins` key of your `project.clj` build configuration (demonstrated below).

Before you can use *lein-cljsbuild*, you'll need to create a Leiningen project (if you don't have one already). In your command console, switch to a directory of your choice, then type:

```
lein new hello-world
```

This will generate a new directory prepopulated with some default files. It should contain a `project.clj` file, which initially will look something like this:

```
(defproject hello-world "0.1.0-SNAPSHOT"
  :description "FIXME: write description"
  :url "http://example.com/FIXME"
  :license {:name "Eclipse Public License"
            :url "http://www.eclipse.org/legal/epl-v10.html"}
  :dependencies [[org.clojure/clojure "1.4.0"]])
```

To enable *lein-cljsbuild*, you'll need to add two lines: a `:plugins` key adding *lein-cljsbuild* to the project, and a `:cljsbuild` key containing build configurations (which will start out empty). Once you've added them, your `project.clj` should look something like the following:

```
(defproject hello-world "0.1.0-SNAPSHOT"
  :description "FIXME: write description"
  :url "http://example.com/FIXME"
  :license {:name "Eclipse Public License"
            :url "http://www.eclipse.org/legal/epl-v10.html"}
  :dependencies [[org.clojure/clojure "1.4.0"]
                 [org.clojure/clojurescript "0.0-1450"]]
  :plugins [[lein-cljsbuild "0.2.7"]]
  :cljsbuild {:builds []})
```

Note that on a new project, you should specify whichever versions of Clojure, Clojure-Script, and *lein-cljsbuild* are most recent (at the time of writing, this is 1.4.0, 0.0-1450, and 0.2.7, respectively, as shown in the example `project.clj`).

Getting Started with the REPL

The fastest way to start writing ClojureScript code is to fire up the REPL. For those not already familiar with the concept of a REPL from Clojure or another Lisp, REPL stands for Read Eval Print Loop, and is similar to a shell console in other languages because it can be used to program interactively. It works by successively reading text input into Lisp data structures, evaluating them in the running environment (via compilation to JavaScript, in ClojureScript's case), printing the results of the expression back to the console, and looping back and waiting for more input.

To start a basic REPL in a *lein-cljsbuild* project, type the following at the command line from anywhere in the project's directory structure:

```
lein trampoline cljsbuild repl-rhino
```

This statement deserves some unpacking:

- `lein` invokes the Leiningen build system.
- `trampoline` is some ceremony Leiningen requires for running tasks with interactive user input in the console.
- `cljsbuild` invokes the *lein-cljsbuild* plug-in.
- `repl-rhino` specifies that you'll use the *Rhino* REPL. Rhino is a headless JavaScript engine that runs on the JVM, which is convenient for basic experimentation with ClojureScript.

Once the REPL starts up, you should see the ClojureScript REPL prompt:

```
ClojureScript:cljs.user>
```

Type a ClojureScript expression (for example, the `println` function to print to standard out in Rhino), and press Enter to evaluate it:

```
ClojureScript:cljs.user> (println "Hello, world!")
Hello, world!
nil
```

You will immediately see the string you specified printed, and the return value of the expression (which is nil, in the case of println).

You can use the Rhino REPL like this to explore any of ClojureScript's basic syntax and standard libraries.

Rhino REPL versus the Browser REPL

ClojureScript actually ships with two REPLs: the Rhino REPL and the Browser REPL. The Rhino REPL is much simpler and easier to use, but runs in a sandboxed, headless JavaScript instance, implemented using Rhino (*http://www.mozilla.org/rhino/*). For basic exploration of ClojureScript and its syntax, it works great.

However, one major use case for ClojureScript is browser programming, and for that, ideally, one wants a REPL that actually runs against a real browser JavaScript environment with full access to the DOM (Document Object Model) and the ability to see changes reflected in a running browser. ClojureScript supports this, but out of necessity the model is slightly more complicated.

The Browser REPL runs as two components: a client, which runs as ClojureScript in a browser, and a server, which is a separate Java process that runs on the developer's machine and exposes an interactive console. The browser client maintains a long polling connection to the server, and whenever the developer enters an expression at the REPL console, it is compiled to JavaScript and sent to the browser, which evaluates the expression and sends back the result.

Full instructions for configuring and using the Browser REPL are included in Chapter 9.

Compiling a ClojureScript File to JavaScript

Structuring the Leiningen project

To add a ClojureScript file to your Leiningen project, you'll want to make a few tweaks to your project directory layout. Initially, your project layout will look something like this:

```
- hello-world/
  - README.md
  - project.clj
  - src/
    - hello_world/
      - core.clj
```

(Note that test files and folders are omitted for clarity, but you should definitely write unit tests wherever appropriate.)

Since this default structure is designed around having only one type of source code (Clojure), you'll want to modify the directory structure slightly, to match the following:

```
- hello-world/
  - README.md
  - project.clj
  - src/
    - clj/
      - hello_world/
        - core.clj
    - cljs/
  - hello_world
    - resources/
      - public/
```

As you can see, the src folder now has two subfolders, one for each type of source code. You'll need to add a :source-paths configuration key to your project.clj file to reflect the new location of the Clojure source code (see the example below for what the new project.clj file will look like). You will also need to create a folder in which to place the compiled JavaScript: resources/public is a common choice.

Updating the project configuration

Then, you must add a build entry in the :cljsbuild configuration map in project.clj:

```
(defproject hello-world "0.1.0-SNAPSHOT"
  :plugins [[lein-cljsbuild "0.2.7"]]
  :dependencies [[org.clojure/clojure "1.4.0"]
                 [org.clojure/clojurescript "0.0-1450"]]
  :source-paths ["src/clj"]
  :cljsbuild {
    :builds [{
      :source-path "src/cljs"
      :compiler {
        :output-to "resources/public/hello.js"
        :optimizations :whitespace
        :pretty-print true}}]})
```

The :source-path key specifies where the build looks for ClojureScript source files, and the :output-to key of the :compiler option map specifies where the ClojureScript compiler will emit compiled JavaScript files. Other compiler options will be explained in more detail in the next chapter: for now, just use the ones provided.

Writing a ClojureScript file

Finally, write a ClojureScript file! You can start with something very simple, intended to be run in a browser. The following ClojureScript file just declares a namespace, and then prints out "Hello World" using the document.write JavaScript function. Place it in a file named hello.cljs in the *src/cljs/hello_world/* folder (named to match the namespace you declared) in your ClojureScript source folder.

```
(ns hello-world.hello)
(.write js/document "<p>Hello, world!</p>")
```

Compiling

Your Leiningen project is now fully configured to compile ClojureScript. Try compiling your ClojureScript by invoking the `lein cljsbuild once` command from the command line, anywhere inside your Leiningen project folder. You should see a status message about successfully compiling `resources/public/hello.js`. If you like, you can inspect the emitted JavaScript file: Be aware, though, that it also includes the core ClojureScript runtime and parts of the standard library, so it's quite long. See the next chapter for details of how this process works.

You might also want to try running `lein cljsbuild auto`. This will keep a process open that will watch all the *.cljs* files in the specified source directories, and whenever one is saved, it will recompile it automatically and replace the output file.

You should also be aware of the `lein cljsbuild clean` command, which will delete all the compiled JavaScript files. By default, *lein-cljsbuild* will not recompile a file unless it detects that the file has been changed by comparing timestamps. Sometimes, however, it's useful to force a recompile by wiping all the compiler output and restarting with a clean slate.

Running ClojureScript in the Browser

If you've written a ClojureScript file as described in the previous section, all you need to do to see it run in a browser is to write an HTML file that includes the emitted JS files in the standard way. It is common practice to place static HTML files in `resources/public`.

```
<html>
<head><title>ClojureScript Hello World</title></head>
<body>
    <script type="text/javascript" src="hello.js"></script>
</body>
</html>
```

Open this file in the browser, and you should see your greeting, as coded in your `hello.cljs` file. If you're running *lein-cljsbuild* in automatic mode, simply edit the message in `hello.cljs`, save the file, and refresh the browser to see your change.

Other Capabilities of lein-cljsbuild

Note that in addition to this basic compilation, *lein-cljsbuild* provides several other useful development tools and options. These include:

- Multiple ClojureScript builds with different options.
- Launching the browser REPL.
- Cross compiling the same code as both Clojure and ClojureScript (provided it meets certain requirements).

See Chapter 9 for full instructions on all the configuration options and features available.

CHAPTER 3

The Compilation Process

ClojureScript has a tight symbiotic relationship with other tools. This chapter will explain how all the different parts fit together and then demonstrate the ClojureScript compilation process.

Architecture

ClojureScript is a compiler—that is, a program that takes a "source" representation as input and emits a "target" representation as output. The source representation of the ClojureScript compiler is the ClojureScript language, and the target representation is JavaScript.

Unlike some JavaScript-generation tools and frameworks, ClojureScript itself does not do any "minification" or other optimizations to reduce the size of the JavaScript code it emits. Instead, ClojureScript is designed to work with the Google Closure Compiler to produce optimized JavaScript.

Google Closure Compiler

The Google Closure Compiler is a free, open-source compiler that uses JavaScript as both source and target representations. That is, it compiles JavaScript into JavaScript. Along the way, it can perform sophisticated optimizations to reduce the size and improve the runtime performance of JavaScript code.

The fact that "Clojure" and "Closure" are homophones is an unfortunate historical accident. The owners/authors of the two projects have no relationship to one another. In this book, we will always refer to the "Google Closure Compiler" and the "Google Closure Library" by their full names.

The Google Closure Compiler can run in three different modes:

Whitespace Only
> This mode removes only comments and unnecessary whitespace from JavaScript source code. The target JavaScript is functionally identical to the source JavaScript. This is similar to some simple JavaScript "minifiers."

Simple Optimizations
> This mode does all the same optimizations as *Whitespace Only* mode and further reduces the size of target JavaScript by renaming local variables and function parameters to shorter names.

Advanced Optimizations
> This mode does all the same optimizations as the previous two modes and also performs aggressive whole-program optimizations of JavaScript code. It will completely remove "dead" or unreachable code, rename functions and global variables to shorter names, and even rename inline function bodies when doing so will save space.

While the more aggressive optimization modes of the compiler can dramatically reduce the size of JavaScript source code, they come with a few caveats. In order to perform the optimizations in *Simple* and *Advanced* modes, the Google Closure Compiler must make certain assumptions about the source JavaScript. If the source JavaScript code violates these assumptions, the Google Closure Compiler will produce target JavaScript code that does not work as intended.

For example, *Simple Optimizations* mode will break JavaScript code that uses JavaScript's `with` operator, `eval` function, or any string representation of function or parameter names. *Advanced Optimizations* mode is even more restrictive: because it renames global variables and functions to shorten their names, it will break any code that depends on names being stable. For example, code that refers to object property names as strings (like `user["name"]` instead of `user.name`) will sometimes break under *Advanced* mode.

The documentation for the Google Closure Compiler explains all the effects of *Advanced Optimizations* mode in detail. Essentially, using the Google Closure Compiler in *Advanced* mode requires that developers follow strict conventions for how their JavaScript code is structured. The JavaScript code that results from following these conventions often looks "unnatural" to developers accustomed to writing optimized JavaScript code by hand, but the final result produced by the Google Closure Compiler is generally just as or more efficient than hand-optimized JavaScript run through a "minifier."

> Google makes a Closure Compiler demo application (*http://closure-compiler.appspot.com/*) available for developers to experiment with the effects of different compilation modes.

The Google Closure Library

The Google Closure Compiler is distributed along with an extensive collection of free and open-source libraries, written in JavaScript, which follow all the conventions required by the compiler in *Advanced Optimizations* mode. These libraries include data structures, common algorithms, abstractions over browser quirks, and even a GUI toolkit. Because of the *Advanced*-mode conventions, the source code of these libraries may look "unnatural" to a JavaScript developer. The Google Closure Library code is written to target the Google Closure Compiler, so it is more verbose than most JavaScript written to target web browsers directly. Common by-hand JavaScript optimizations, such as using short names for common functions, do not matter in *Advanced* mode, because the compiler will rename everything anyway.

The Google Closure Library is much larger than most JavaScript libraries—several megabytes as opposed to a few hundred kilobytes. Again, a JavaScript developer accustomed to hand-optimized code would think this is grossly inefficient. But the Google Closure Compiler's *Advanced*-mode optimizations ensure the actual code delivered in a production application is much smaller. Any "dead" library code not actually used by the application will be eliminated during compilation. In short, you only pay (in download size) for what you use.

A Few Words on Caching

The Google Closure Compiler is designed to reduce the *overall* download size of your application, but it does not facilitate re-use of JavaScript libraries across different applications in the same client. Experienced JavaScript developers may be more accustomed to fetching popular JavaScript libraries from Content Delivery Networks (CDNs) and relying on browser caches to reduce the overall download size. But caching is not a panacea (see Sam Saffron's article, "Stop paying your jQuery tax (*http://samsaffron.com/archive/2012/02/17/stop-paying-your-jquery-tax*)"):

- Many users will not have the library in their cache.
- Even if a library is in the cache, web browsers will still perform an HTTP request to make sure the cache is up to date.
- Parsing and executing a large JavaScript library takes time, even in the fastest browsers.

As with any performance optimization problem, only exhaustive testing can prove which method is more efficient overall. Using the Google Closure Compiler, you can still utilize CDNs and client-side caching for the application code itself. Given the growing diversity of JavaScript libraries and applications, this seems like a good approach. Google itself has used this technique to deploy large, complex browser applications such as GMail and Google Docs.

ClojureScript and Google Closure

ClojureScript is designed to work with the Google Closure Compiler and Library. The ClojureScript compiler emits JavaScript code that is fully compatible with the *Advanced Optimizations* mode of the Google Closure Compiler. As a result, when programming in ClojureScript you rarely need to think about the JavaScript conventions required by *Advanced* mode. Many of the core libraries included with ClojureScript make use of functions in the Google Closure Library.

Using ClojureScript does not mean that you are restricted to using code only in the Google Closure Library. ClojureScript can make use of any JavaScript library with a little additional configuration. However, most hand-optimized JavaScript libraries are *not* written with the Google Closure Compiler in mind, so they will not be compatible with *Advanced Optimizations* mode. ClojureScript can still use libraries such as jQuery or Prototype, but the libraries themselves will not receive the benefit of *Advanced*-mode compilation. Chapter 7 will cover using third-party JavaScript libraries in ClojureScript.

The Compilation Pipeline

The final picture of ClojureScript compilation looks like Figure 3-1.

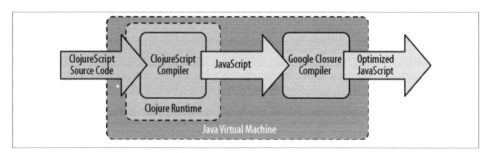

Figure 3-1. ClojureScript Compilation Process

The entire compilation process happens inside a Java Virtual Machine (JVM), presumably running on a server or developer's machine. The ClojureScript compiler is written in the Clojure language, which runs on the JVM. The Google Closure Compiler is written in the Java language.

The ClojureScript compiler takes ClojureScript source code and compiles it into unoptimized JavaScript, which it passes to the Google Closure Compiler along with JavaScript libraries. The Google Closure Compiler takes in all the unoptimized JavaScript and emits a single optimized JavaScript source file.

The JavaScript output by the Google Closure Compiler in *Advanced Optimizations* mode is intended for consumption by JavaScript execution engines, not humans. It is not readable and not very suitable for JavaScript debugging tools. When developing your application, it is more common to omit the Google Closure Compiler from the compilation process, which will result in readable JavaScript. Function and variable names in the emitted JavaScript can easily be correlated with sources in ClojureScript. Debugging support in ClojureScript still has room for improvement, but the process is already usable. In addition, ClojureScript has some unique debugging tools such as the browser-connected Read-Eval-Print-Loop (REPL), which we will cover in Chapter 9.

How to Compile

In this section, we will walk through the ClojureScript compilation process in detail, showing how the parts interact.

The Java Classpath

Most programming language implementations assume that source code libraries will be installed in some standard location, accessible system-wide. Java is different. Every time you launch the JVM, you must explicitly specify a *classpath*, a list of directories and files to search when loading code. The classpath is fixed when the JVM starts and cannot be changed while it is running. (Technically, it is possible to manipulate the classpath using *classloaders*, an esoteric JVM feature that is far outside the scope of this book.)

Most Java libraries are published as Java Archive (JAR) files. JAR files are simply compressed files in the ZIP format with some additional metadata. The Clojure runtime, the ClojureScript compiler, and the Google Closure Compiler are all distributed as JAR files. (You can find links to download the JAR files at the Central Maven Repository (*http://search.maven.org/*), the most widely-used repository of JAR files. Search for "clojurescript" or "google closure" to find the latest releases.) In addition, the ClojureScript authors have packaged and distributed a version of the Google Closure Library as a JAR file for convenience.

Although it is possible to launch the Java Virtual Machine and specify the classpath directly from the command line, this is rarely done in practice. Managing the classpath is one of the principal concerns of build tools, IDEs, and application servers targeting the Java language. Clojure has its own such tool, Leiningen, which was introduced in Chapter 2 and will be covered further in Chapter 9.

Compiling ClojureScript

The entire ClojureScript build chain, including the ClojureScript compiler and the Google Closure Compiler, can be invoked as a single function in Clojure. In this section, we will use the Clojure REPL to explore the various options of the ClojureScript compiler. We'll use a variant of the "Hello, World" example from Chapter 2. Instead of using *lein-cljsbuild*, this example will invoke the ClojureScript compiler directly. This process is unlikely to become part of your day-to-day development workflow, but it is helpful to understand how the parts work. You can also use this section as a guide to incorporating ClojureScript into customized builds.

Hello, Compiler

Create a new project like this:

```
lein new ch03-hello-compiler
```

Then modify the `project.clj` file to look like this:

```
(defproject ch03-hello-compiler "0.1.0-SNAPSHOT"
  :dependencies [[org.clojure/clojure "1.4.0"]
                 [org.clojure/clojurescript "0.0-1450"]]
  :source-paths ["src/clj"])
```

Create the `src/clj` and `src/cljs` directories as in Chapter 2, then put the following ClojureScript source file in `src/cljs/hello_compiler/hello.cljs`:

```
(ns hello-compiler.hello)

(defn ^:export main []
  (.write js/document "<p>Hello, ClojureScript compiler!</p>"))
```

Finally, create an HTML file at *public/resources/index.html*:

```
<!DOCTYPE html>
<html>
<head><title>ClojureScript Hello Compiler</title></head>
<body>
    <script src="hello.js" type="text/javascript"></script>
    <script>hello_compiler.hello.main()</script>
</body>
</html>
```

The Clojure REPL

Both Clojure and ClojureScript have their own REPLs. In this chapter, we are going to invoke the ClojureScript compiler, which is implemented in Clojure, so we will be using the *Clojure* REPL. In your new project, you can launch the Clojure REPL by running:

```
lein repl
```

Then type the following to load the ClojureScript compiler:

```
(require 'cljs.closure)
```

Then type the following (long) expression to compile your project with the Google Closure Compiler in *Advanced Mode*:

```
(cljs.closure/build "src/cljs"
  {:output-to "resources/public/hello.js"
   :optimizations :advanced})
```

The *Advanced Mode* optimizations are time-consuming: this simple build may take 20 seconds or more. When it finishes, you will have an optimized JavaScript source file at `resources/public/hello.js`. Compare the size of this file with the unoptimized file you created in Chapter 2—the optimized JavaScript emitted by the Google Closure Compiler is much smaller.

Compilation in Depth

When you type (`cljs.closure/build ...`) in the Clojure REPL you are invoking a function. The entire function call is wrapped in parentheses. The `cljs.closure/build` function takes two arguments, a *source* and a *map* of *options*:

```
(cljs.closure/build source options-map)
```

Compilation Sources

The *source* argument tells the compiler where to find our ClojureScript source files. Typically, it is the name of a directory, given as a string. The compiler will find all files with the `.cljs` extension in that directory and compile them together.

The *source* argument can also be the name of a single file to be compiled. This might be useful during development, when you only want to recompile part of a project.

Compilation and Optimization Options

The *options* are passed to the `cljs.closure/build` function in a Clojure *map*, written as a series of pairs inside curly braces.

In the previous example, we passed two options:

```
:output-to      "resources/public/hello.js"
:optimizations  :advanced
```

The words that begin with colons are *keywords*, a special kind of literal data in Clojure and ClojureScript. For our purposes, they act like constants.

:optimizations

We have already seen two possible values for the `:optimizations` option, in this and the previous chapter. This option controls the optimization mode in which to run the Google Closure Compiler.

`:optimizations` Value	Google Closure Compiler Mode
:none	(disabled)
:whitespace	*Whitespace-Only*
:simple	*Simple Optimizations*
:advanced	*Advanced Optimizations*

With an `:optimizations` value of `:none`, the Google Closure Compiler will not be invoked at all, and the build will write out the JavaScript produced by the ClojureScript compiler directly. This mode is useful for development and debugging. However, the JavaScript output will be split across many individual files, requiring slightly different handling in a browser (more on this later).

Where do the files go?

The ClojureScript compiler produces one JavaScript file for each ClojureScript source file. These files go in a directory controlled by the `:output-dir` option, which defaults to a directory named `out` in the current working directory. The current working directory is whatever directory the Java (or Leiningen) process was started in. The JVM does not support changing the current working directory once a program has started.

The Google Closure Compiler is designed to optimize JavaScript for delivery over slow networks. As a consequence, it always produces a *single* JavaScript file for the entire compiled application. When any one of the optimization modes is enabled, the output of `cljs.closure/build` will always be a single JavaScript file.

Compiling with optimizations

Figure 3-2 shows the behavior of the `cljs.closure/build` function when compiling with optimizations. The `:output-dir` option controls where the ClojureScript compiler writes intermediate files. The `:output-to` option specifies the file location of the final output from the Google Closure Compiler. When you are compiling your application for production use, this is the JavaScript file you would put on your web server and reference in HTML pages.

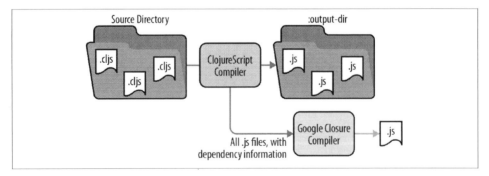

Figure 3-2. Compiler inputs and outputs with optimization

If you do not specify an output file, the `cljs.closure/build` function simply returns the compiled JavaScript source code as one giant string. This might be interesting if you want to understand how the compiler works, but it's still going to be a big blob of your entire application, so it's probably not useful.

Loading optimized code in a browser

To run your optimized code in a browser, simply include the :output-to file in a <script> tag, like this:

```
<script src="hello.js" type="text/javascript"></script>
```

ClojureScript programs usually do not act like "scripts" in the conventional sense. Loading the compiled JavaScript does not *do* anything except define functions. You typically launch your application with a "main" or "start" function invoked in a separate <script> tag, like this:

```
<script>
  hello_compiler.hello.main();
</script>
```

The details of how the ClojureScript function names translate to JavaScript object names will be covered in more detail in Chapter 7, but the short version is that hyphens become underscores.

Compiling without optimizations

When you specify :optimizations :none the Google Closure Compiler does not run at all (Figure 3-3). But the :output-to option is still important.

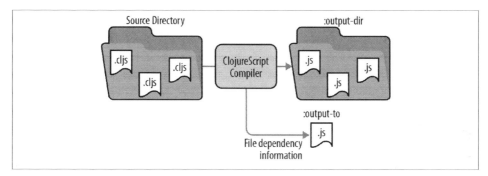

Figure 3-3. Compiler inputs and outputs without optimization

The Google Closure Library includes a dependency-resolution feature that makes it possible to split a JavaScript application across many source files and automatically load the right files in a web browser. This mechanism will be covered in detail in Chapter 7. For now, just know that the dependency resolution mechanism requires a special file that declares all the dependency relationships in your source code. When compiling *without* optimizations, the ClojureScript compiler writes this information to the file specified by the :output-to option.

In order for a browser to load the individual files, the `:output-dir` option must be set to a directory that you can reference in the `<script>` tag of an HTML file. In our examples, the convention is `"resources/public/js"`.

Loading unoptimized code in a browser

To run your application in a browser without optimizations, you need *four* `<script>` tags in your HTML, in precisely this order:

```
<script src="js/goog/base.js"></script>
<script src="hello.js"></script>
<script> goog.require('hello_compiler.hello'); </script>
<script> hello_compiler.hello.main(); </script>
```

The first `<script>` tag loads the Google Closure Library from `goog/base.js`, which will be found in the directory specified by the `:output-dir` option.

The second `<script>` tag loads the dependency information for your application from the file specified by the `:output-to` option.

The third `<script>` tag uses the Google Closure Library function `goog.require` to load your application. The argument to `goog.require` is a JavaScript string naming the primary *namespace* of your application. Namespaces will be fully covered in Chapter 7, but you have already seen them in all of the code examples. The ClojureScript expression (ns `hello-compiler.hello`) declares a namespace named `hello-compiler.hello`. Once again, hyphens become underscores in JavaScript, yielding `hello_compiler.hel lo`.

The fourth `<script>` tag launches your application, the same as in the optimized case. Because of the way `goog.require` works, the code to launch your application *must* be in a separate `<script>` tag coming *after* the `<script>` that calls `goog.require`.

An alternative: pretty-printing

In general, you will compile your ClojureScript application for production with `:opti mizations :advanced`, and for development with `:optimizations :none`. But there is a third way, which is to use `:optimizations :whitespace` and also add the `:pretty- print true` option. This combination will still combine all of your JavaScript into a single source file and invoke the Google Closure Compiler, but it will reformat the JavaScript code for maximum readability.

The compilation process with `:optimizations :whitespace` and `:pretty-print true` takes slightly longer than with `:optimizations :none`, but it has the advantage of being simpler to use. You can use the exact same HTML `<script>` tags that you would use for fully-optimized production code, but you can still read and debug the JavaScript code directly in the browser.

The pretty-printing feature is provided by the Google Closure Compiler, so it has no effect with :optimizations :none.

Other Compilation Options

The default target for the ClojureScript compiler is web browsers. The compiler can also be used to emit JavaScript code for other execution environments, such as Node.js.[1] Passing the option :target :nodejs to cljs.closure/build will tell the ClojureScript compiler to emit code, which is compatible with *Node.js*. Compiling ClojureScript for *Node.js* is still an experimental feature and not widely used, so we do not cover it in this book.

The :libs, :foreign-libs, and :externs options control access to external JavaScript libraries; these will be covered in Chapter 7.

Summary

All the compilation options to cljs.closure/build are summarized in Table 3-1.

Table 3-1. Compilation options

Option	Possible Values
:output-to	file path as a string
:output-dir	directory path as a string
:optimizations	:none, :whitespace, :advanced
:pretty-print	false (default), true
:target	(browsers by default), :nodejs
:libs	See Chapter 7.
:foreign-libs	See Chapter 7.
:externs	See Chapter 7.

This chapter explained the high-level architecture ClojureScript compiler and its relationship with the Google Closure Compiler. We showed how to launch the Clojure and ClojureScript REPLs and how to invoke the ClojureScript compiler.

In subsequent chapters we will delve into the ClojureScript language itself. The Clojure/ClojureScript REPL shown in Chapter 2 and Chapter 3 should be sufficient to follow along with the examples that follow. After covering the language, we will circle back to compilation and development workflow in more detail.

1. *http://nodejs.org/*

CHAPTER 4

ClojureScript Basics

ClojureScript is a simple language, which is to say that it is based on a small number of fundamental concepts. If you have only written programs in imperative, object-oriented languages such as Java, C++, and JavaScript, then some of these concepts may be unfamiliar to you at first. However, by learning those concepts, you will be rewarded with a powerful new programming tool.

ClojureScript versus Clojure

At the language level, ClojureScript is designed to mimic Clojure as much as possible. However, neither ClojureScript nor Clojure makes any attempt to hide operational details of the underlying host platform, JavaScript or the JVM, respectively. As a result, there will be differences between the two languages wherever their host platforms are involved:

- Calls to host methods or classes
- Built-in types such as strings and numbers
- Built-in operations such as arithmetic
- Concurrency and threading (JavaScript is single-threaded)
- Performance

At this time, ClojureScript does not implement all of the Clojure language. In particular, ClojureScript does not include most of the concurrency features for which Clojure is so well known; because JavaScript VMs are single-threaded, these features are less important. There are also features of Clojure that have not yet been implemented in ClojureScript simply because work has not yet been completed.

Clojure itself is a young programming language (first released in 2007) but it has grown rapidly in stability, ease of use, and performance. ClojureScript is even younger (first released in 2011) and is consequentially less mature. You can expect to find rough edges, bugs, and undocumented features. While we hope that this book will help to ameliorate the latter, nothing can take the place of experience that comes from building real-world applications.

This book does not attempt to fully document all the features of the Clojure language, or even all of the features currently implemented in ClojureScript. Instead, we will attempt to provide enough to get you started and working productively in ClojureScript. When you are ready to learn more, there are many books available on the Clojure language: most of their material will apply equally well to ClojureScript.

Expressions and Side Effects

Most mainstream programming languages, including JavaScript, have both *statements* and *expressions*. In JavaScript, statements end with a semicolon (usually) and are typically related to flow control: for, if, while, and so on. JavaScript expressions include literals (numbers, strings, regexes), function calls, and arithmetic operations. The key difference is that expressions always have a *value* whereas statements do not. Expressions can be nested: you can place a function call expression inside an if statement, but not the other way around.

In ClojureScript, everything is an expression and everything has a value, even the control structures. (Sometimes that value is null, but it's still a value.) You can even define your own flow-control expressions using *macros*, which we will cover in Chapter 8. The process of going from an expression to its value is called *evaluating* the expression.

Some expressions can have *side effects*, things that happen when they are evaluated other than simply returning a value. Printing output to the screen or manipulating an HTML document in a web browser are both side effects. ClojureScript favors a "functional" style of programming in which most code consists of "pure" expressions that return a value with no side effects. Of course, a program entirely without side effects cannot produce any output at all, so ClojureScript allows you to break out of the functional style when you need to.

Syntax and Data Structures

As we said, everything in ClojureScript is an expression, including the primitive data types, which "evaluate" to themselves. Comments begin with a semicolon and continue to the end of a line.

```
42, 3.14159          ; Numbers
"Hello, World!"      ; String
#"\d{3}-\d{3}-\d{4}" ; RegExp
true, false          ; Boolean
nil                  ; null
```

ClojureScript numbers and strings are the same as JavaScript Number and String objects, with essentially the same syntax. ClojureScript regular expressions evaluate to JavaScript RegExp but have slightly different syntax.

Symbols and Keywords

```
map, +, swap!   ; Symbols
:meta, :my-id   ; Keywords
```

ClojureScript has *symbols*, which are just bare words in your program. Symbols evaluate to other values, such as functions, and also serve a role similar to local variables, although they are not really variables. The *name* of a symbol can contain almost any character, including hyphens and other punctuation. Things that are typically special operators in other languages, such as the arithmetic operators +, -, *, and /, are just symbols in ClojureScript, which evaluate to the built-in arithmetic functions.

ClojureScript also has *keywords*, written as symbols with a leading colon. Keywords always evaluate to themselves. Unlike symbols, they never stand in for anything else. In JavaScript, strings are often used for constants or identifiers in code; keywords fill the same role in ClojureScript.

Data Structures

```
(1 2 3), (print "Hello")  ; Lists
[:a :b :c 1 2 3]          ; Vector
{:a 1, "b" 2}             ; Map
#{3 7 :z}                 ; Set
```

Finally, there are the four basic data structures. Vectors, maps, and sets evaluate to themselves: they are literal data structures similar to JavaScript's arrays and objects. Individual elements in a data structure must be separated by whitespace. In Clojure-Script, commas count as whitespace in addition to the usual space, tab, and line break. We will talk more about these data structures in the next chapter.

Lists can be used as literal data, but more often they are used to construct expressions. When the ClojureScript compiler encounters a list, it examines the first element of the list and tries to invoke it. The first element is the *function position* of the list. It is usually a symbol naming a function, but it could also be a macro or special operator, which we will define later.

Even operators like + and * are functions, so they must appear in function position. ClojureScript code therefore uses *prefix notation* instead of the more common *algebraic notation* used by most programming languages. In ClojureScript, the parentheses are always required, but there are no "operator precedence" rules to remember:

```
(+ 9 (* 10 5))   ; 9 + 10 * 5 in algebraic notation
```

As for syntax, that's (almost) all there is to it! Everything in ClojureScript is composed from these simple parts.

The following expression contains two lists, one nested inside the other:

```
(println (+ 3 4))
```

The outer list contains two elements: the symbol `println` in function position and the inner list. The inner list has the symbol + in function position, followed by two numbers.

Expressions are evaluated from the inside out, so this example will compile into JavaScript code, which adds 3 to 4 and then prints the result. Printing is a side effect; the whole expression *evaluates* to `nil`, which is the value returned by the `println` function. If you type this expression into the ClojureScript REPL, you will see 7 printed on one line and `nil` on the following line.

Special Forms and Definitions

As we mentioned in the previous section, the symbol in the function position of a list may be a function, macro, or special operator. Special operators are symbols that are defined by the ClojureScript compiler. These are the "primitives" of the language, and there are only a handful you will encounter, such as `if`, `def`, and `do`. Most of the standard operators in ClojureScript, such as arithmetic and control flow, are handled by functions and macros.

One special operator you will use often is `def`, which defines a new *binding* from a symbol to a value. After a new binding is created with `def`, evaluating the symbol will return its value.

For example, here we bind the symbol `my-name` to a string:

```
(def my-name "Leslie Q. Coder")
```

Symbol bindings created with `def` compile into JavaScript `var` declarations, but you should think of them as constants, not local variables. In particular, `def` expressions are not intended to be used inside functions, nor should they be used to rebind symbols to new values (except during interactive development at the REPL).

Functions

ClojureScript functions are very much like JavaScript functions. The `fn` macro creates unnamed, *anonymous* functions, like JavaScript's `function` operator.

The `fn` symbol appears in function position of a list, followed by the *parameters* (arguments) to the function as a vector of symbols, followed by one or more expressions comprising the *body* of the function. Here is a simple function:

```
(fn [name] (str "Hello, " name))
```

This function takes one argument, called `name`, and calls the `str` function, which concatenates strings, in its body. It compiles to JavaScript that looks something like this:

```
function(name) { return cljs.core.str("Hello, " name); }
```

A function isn't very useful unless we can call it. Remember that the first element of a list is evaluated as a function, so we can place a literal `fn` at the front of a list to invoke it. The arguments we want to pass to the function are the remaining elements of the list:

```
((fn [name] (str "Hello, " name)) "ClojureScript")
;;=> "Hello, ClojureScript"
```

This example compiles to JavaScript that creates an anonymous function and immediately invokes it, like this:

```
(function(name) {
    return cljs.core.str("Hello, " name);
})("ClojureScript");
```

Even this is not very practical, so we usually want to give our functions names. Functions are values like any other, so we can use the `def` macro to bind them to symbols. Here we bind the symbol `greeting` to a function and then call it by name:

```
(def greeting
  (fn [name] (str "Hello, " name)))

(greeting "functions!")
;;=> "Hello, functions!"
```

Binding symbols to functions is so common that ClojureScript has a macro to make it easier. The `defn` macro takes a symbol to define, followed by the parameter vector and function body as with `fn`.

```
(defn greeting [name]
  (str "Hello, " name))
```

We will explore macros further in Chapter 8. For now, just know that they can control the way things are evaluated.

Multi-Arity Functions

In JavaScript, any function can be called with any number of arguments, and those arguments can be accessed via the `arguments` array. ClojureScript allows functions to be defined with several *arities*, or numbers of arguments. Each arity of the function can have different behavior. A multi-arity function looks like this:

```
(defn greeting
  ([] (greeting "Hello" "world"))
  ([name] (greeting "Hello" name))
  ([salutation name] (str salutation ", " name "!")))
```

Each arity of the function is its own list inside the function definition. The first element of each list is the argument vector, followed by the function body. This example demonstrates a common use of multi-arity functions: to provide default values for some or all of the parameters. Multi-arity functions may feel similar to "function overloading" in languages such as C and Java, with the difference that they are overloaded only on the number, not the type, of their arguments.

Variadic Functions

In addition to having multiple arities, a ClojureScript function can be defined to take any number of arguments: this is called a *variadic* function. A variadic function has the special symbol & (ampersand) before the last symbol in its argument vector, as in the following:

```
(defn average
  ([x] x)
  ([x y] (/ (+ x y) 2))
  ([x y & extra] (/ (reduce + (+ x y) extra)
                    (+ 2 (count extra)))))
```

This example defines a function with three arities, the last of which is variadic. If the `average` function is called with one argument, it returns that argument. If it is called with two arguments, it adds them together and divides by 2. If it is called with three *or more* arguments, it computes their average using the `reduce` and `count` functions, which we will cover in Chapter 6. Notice that a function can be both multi-arity and variadic at the same time, but only one of a function's arities can be variadic.

Local Bindings

ClojureScript does not have variables like JavaScript because all data is immutable, but it does permit you to create a *local binding* between a symbol and a value with the `let` expression, as shown below:

```
(let [binding-form value-expr
      ...]
  ... expressions ...)
```

The let expression begins with a vector of *bindings*. Each binding is a pair: first a *binding form*, usually a symbol, then a *value expression*. When evaluated, the let evaluates the value expressions, in order, and binds them to the symbols in the binding forms. This creates a local binding within the body of the let. For example:

```
(let [x 4
      y (+ x 3)]
  (println "The product of" x "and" y "is")
  (println (* x y)))
;; The product of 4 and 7 is
;; 28
;;=> nil
```

Notice that the value expressions can include references to the symbols created in earlier bindings.

Destructuring

In addition to symbols, binding forms can include data structures such as vectors and maps. The result of the value expression will be *destructured* to match the binding form. For example:

```
(def nums (list 2 3 5 8 13 21))

(let [[a b c & the-rest] nums]
  (println "a is" a)
  (println "b is" b)
  (println "c is" c)
  (println "the-rest is" the-rest))
;; a is 2
;; b is 3
;; c is 5
;; the-rest is (8 13 21)
```

In this example, the binding form is the vector [a b c & the-rest]. It destructures the list nums and assigns a to 2, b to 3, and so on. The special symbol & collects all the remaining elements into a list and binds it to the following symbol, the-rest.

The full syntax of destructuring is a rich and powerful mini-language of its own; refer to the Clojure language documentation for more details and examples.

Closures

Like JavaScript, ClojureScript supports *lexical closures*. A function can refer to symbols defined in the *lexical scope* in which it was created. Function arguments and the let form create lexical scopes. For example:

```
(defn make-adder [n]
  (fn [x] (+ x n)))
```

```
(def add4 (make-adder 4))
(def add7 (make-adder 7))

(add4 10)
;;=> 14

(add7 10)
;;=> 17
```

In this example, the make-adder function returns another function which "closes over" the value of n in its scope. We can use make-adder to define new functions add4 and add7, which "remember" the binding of n that was in effect when they were created.

Flow Control

As we said at the start of this chapter, everything is an expression in ClojureScript. That includes the control-flow expressions. For our purposes, a flow-control expression is one that controls how its components are evaluated. For example, an if expression is only going to evaluate one branch. This is what makes if different from a function call, which always evaluates all of its arguments.

This section introduces some of the most common flow-control expressions in ClojureScript. Some of them are special forms defined in the compiler, and some are macros defined in the core library, but the difference doesn't matter at this point.

Conditional Branching

In ClojureScript, the basic conditional branch is represented by an if expression:

```
(if test-expr
    then-expr
    else-expr)
```

The if expression takes three subexpressions. First, it will evaluate the *test-expr*. If the result of the *test-expr* is *logical true* (see the sidebar on "Truthiness"), then it will evaluate the *then-expr*, otherwise it will evaluate the *else-expr*. For example:

```
(if (even? 42)
    (println "42 is even")
    (println "42 is odd"))
```

Truthiness

What is logical true? In ClojureScript, nil, false, and the undefined value (written js/undefined) are logical false, and *anything else* is logical true. This is different from JavaScript, which also considers 0, NaN, and the empty string to be logical false.

```
(if false :truthy :falsey)             ;=> :falsey
(if nil :truthy :falsey)               ;=> :falsey
(if js/undefined :truthy :falsey)      ;=> :falsey

(if true :truthy :falsey)              ;=> :truthy
(if 0 :truthy :falsey)                 ;=> :truthy
(if "" :truthy :falsey)                ;=> :truthy
(if js/NaN :truthy :falsey)            ;=> :truthy
(if [] :truthy :falsey)                ;=> :truthy
```

Different programming languages have different ideas of truth. In C, 0 is false and any other number is true. Java has the primitive boolean type, which can be either true or false. ClojureScript's definition of logical truth is consistent with Clojure (except js/undefined, which has no equivalent in Clojure). Using nil as a logical false value is useful in the context of sequences, which are covered in Chapter 6.

The js/NaN value is JavaScript's "not a number," resulting from calculations like zero divided by zero. js/NaN is never equal to anything, including itself:

```
(if (= js/NaN js/NaN) :yes :no)     ;=> :no
```

cond

It is possible to create multiple branches with nested if expressions, but it is more concise to use the cond macro instead:

```
(cond test-expr-1 body-expr-1
      test-expr-2 body-expr-2
      ...
      :else else-expr)
```

The cond macro contains matched pairs of test and body expressions. It evaluates each test expression in order. If one of the test expressions returns logical true, then cond evaluates the matching body expression and returns. If none of the test expressions returns logical true, then cond returns nil.

It is possible to add a "default" case to a cond expression by using the keyword :else as a test expression. Since :else is a keyword, it evaluates to itself, and because it is neither nil nor false, it is always logical true. In fact, any logical true value would work, but it is conventional to use the keyword :else.

As an example, here is a conditional written first with nested if expressions and then with cond:

```
(if (<= x 10)
  "x is a small number"
  (if (<= 11 x 100)
    "x is a medium-sized number"
    (if (<= 101 x 1000)
      "x is a big number"
      "x is a REALLY big number")))
```

```
(cond (<= x 10)
      "x is a small number"
      (<= 11 x 100)
      "x is a medium-sized number"
      (<= 101 x 1000)
      "x is a big number"
      :else
      "x is a REALLY big number")
```

The < and >= functions are the numeric less-than and greater-than-or-equal-to comparisons. Like all other functions in ClojureScript, they must be in function position, so the expression (< x 10) can be read "is x less than 10?" The expression (< 100 x 10000) can be read "is 100 less than x and x less than 10,000?"

Remember that whitespace is never significant in ClojureScript. The test and body expressions in the cond macro can be on the same line or on different lines. All that matters is the order in which they appear.

do

Each body inside an if or cond expression is limited to a single expression. Most of the time, when writing "pure" functions without side effects, this is sufficient. But sometimes side effects are necessary. ClojureScript's do expression allows multiple expressions to be used in the place of one:

```
(do
 ... expressions ...
 )
```

The do form contains any number of expressions. When evaluated, it evaluates each expression in order. It is similar to JavaScript's curly braces {}, except that it also returns a value. The return value of the last expression inside the do block is the return value of the entire do expression.

You can use a do expression to write multiple expressions in a place that normally only takes one expression. This is commonly used when you need to write expressions that have side effects:

```
(cond (< x 10)
      (do (println "x is a small number")
          :small)
      (< 100 x 1000)
      (do (println "x is a big number")
          :big)
      (>= x 10000)
      (do (println "x is a REALLY big number")
          :huge)
      :else
      (do (println  "x is just a medium-sized number")
          :medium))
```

If the value of x is less than 10, this expression will print "x is a small number" *and then return* the keyword :small; if x is between 100 and 10,000, it will print "x is a big number" *and then return* the keyword :big; and so on.

when

ClojureScript provides several built-in macros that combine conditional expressions with an *implicit* do form. This includes the defn macro for defining functions. As another example, the when macro combines the if and do expressions:

```
(when condition
  ... expressions ...)

;; is the same as
(if condition
  (do ... expressions ...))
```

JavaScript Interop

ClojureScript, like Clojure, is designed to stay as close as possible to the semantics of its host platform, only adding to them where necessary. So ClojureScript strings are Java-Script String objects, ClojureScript numbers are JavaScript Number objects, and ClojureScript functions are JavaScript Function objects. You can call JavaScript functions, methods, and constructors just like calling any other function in ClojureScript.

The js Namespace

JavaScript, regrettably, has no concept of *namespaces*. Every function or variable defined in a JavaScript program lives in the same global scope. When two libraries want to use the same name, they often clash. Workarounds exist, such as using JavaScript objects as "modules" and defining things within the scope of anonymous functions, but they are just workarounds.

ClojureScript has built-in support for namespaces at the language level: this is one of the places where it extends the semantics of the host platform to provide a better developer experience. We will cover namespaces more completely in Chapter 7 but one namespace deserves special attention: the js namespace. ClojureScript uses the js namespace to refer to the global scope of a JavaScript program. Core JavaScript constructors such as String and Date are accessed through this namespace, as are browser-defined objects such as window. The following sections show examples of these.

Methods and Fields

ClojureScript can access methods and fields of JavaScript objects directly. A JavaScript method invocation is written in ClojureScript as a list beginning with the method name, prefixed with a . (period). A field access is written similarly but prefixed with a .- (period and hyphen):

```
// JavaScript
var message = "Hello, World!"
var msg_length = message.length;
var insult = message.replace(/World/, "idiots");

;; ClojureScript
(def message "Hello, World!")
(def msg-length (.-length message))
(def insult (.replace message #"World" "idiots"))
```

 In Clojure on the JVM, the same (.name object) syntax was used for both method calls and field accesses. Since the Java language does not allow a method and a field in the same class to have the same name, there was never any ambiguity as to which was intended. But in JavaScript, methods are also fields with functions as values. To prevent ambiguity when calling methods from ClojureScript, the (.-field object) syntax was added for fields. This syntax was later backported to Clojure on the JVM, first appearing in release 1.4.0. Clojure on the JVM still accepts the (.name object) syntax for both fields and methods, but ClojureScript always treats (.name object) as a method call and (.-name object) as a field access.

Notice that the syntaxes for field access and method calls are unified with ClojureScript's syntax for function calls. The "target object" on which a method or field is called no longer has a special position before the method or field name; it becomes just another argument in the function call. Method and field names are not given a namespace qualifier like js/ because they are already scoped within an object.

Constructor Functions

JavaScript constructor functions are also written as lists, but with a . (period or full stop) *appended* to the name of the function:

```
// JavaScript
var today = new Date(2012, 6, 16);

;; ClojureScript
(def today (js/Date. 2012 6 16))
```

Notice that the Date constructor is accessed through the js namespace, written js/Date. The period in js/Date. (with no space in between the period and the function name) tells the ClojureScript compiler that this expression should compile to JavaScript's new operator.

Some built-in JavaScript functions, such as Number and Date, can be called as either a constructor function or an ordinary function. Without the trailing period, the same function can be invoked as an ordinary function, without the new operator:

```javascript
// JavaScript
var today = Date();
```

```clojure
;; ClojureScript
(def today (js/Date))
```

Scope of this

Because of JavaScript's lack of namespaces, it is common practice to attach global functions to "module objects." These functions can be invoked using *either* the namespace-qualified syntax or method call syntax. For example, if you were using the RaphaelJS library,[1] you could call its color function like this:

```javascript
// JavaScript
var green = Raphael.color("#00ff00");
```

```clojure
;; ClojureScript
(def green (Raphael/color "#00ff00"))
```

You could also invoke the color function as a method on the Raphael object in the global JavaScript scope, like this:

```clojure
(defn green (.color js/Raphael "#00ff00"))
```

The difference comes in the handling of JavaScript's this. The namespace-style syntax (Raphael/color) will compile to code that calls the color function with this bound to null. The method-style syntax (.color) will invoke the color function with this bound to the Raphael object. The former is more natural in ClojureScript code, but some JavaScript libraries depend on methods being invoked with this bound to the "module" object.

Functions defined in JavaScript's global scope, such as web browsers' built-in alert() function, are accessed through the js namespace, as shown below. (Note that this example may not work in Microsoft Internet Explorer, because IE's JavaScript implementation defines alert as a special syntactic form, not a normal JavaScript function.)

```javascript
// JavaScript
alert("Hello, World!");
```

1. *http://raphaeljs.com/*

```
;; ClojureScript
(js/alert "Hello, World!")
```

Exceptions

ClojureScript has try/catch/finally and throw forms that behave similarly to their JavaScript equivalents. The try/catch/finally form looks like this:

```
(try
  ;; ... body expressions ...
  (catch ErrClass err
    ;; ... handle an exception of type ErrClass ...
    ;; ... the exception object is bound to err ...
    )
  (catch js/Error err
    ;; ... handle an exception of type Error ...
    )
  (finally
    ;; ... always execute this ...
    ))
```

Both the catch and finally blocks are optional. Note that catch in ClojureScript takes a "class" (constructor function) and only handles exceptions of that class. You can have multiple catch blocks to handle different types of exceptions. This mimics the exception-handling behavior of Clojure on the JVM.

The throw form takes an exception object and throws it:

```
(throw (js/Error. "Houston, we have a problem."))
```

Although JavaScript and ClojureScript both permit you to throw primitives such as strings, this is not recommended. When using JavaScript exception types such as Error, you will need to qualify them in both throw and catch expressions as js/Error.

Summary

This chapter covered the essential syntax of the ClojureScript language. Most of this material is identical to Clojure on the JVM. We have not covered every kind of expression possible in ClojureScript, but any documentation written for Clojure on the JVM should apply equally well to ClojureScript.

JavaScript is already a dynamically-typed language with first-class functions, so some of these features may not be as unfamiliar to JavaScript programmers as they are for programmers accustomed to statically-typed languages such as Java.

There are many more features of the ClojureScript language that we did not have time to cover in this book. For example, multimethods, protocols, and records provide powerful mechanisms for polymorphism. These features are the same in both ClojureScript and Clojure, and there are many resources for them both online and in print.

CHAPTER 5

Data and State

As discussed earlier, ClojureScript is a member of the functional family of programming languages, meaning that the function is the primary unit of abstraction and composition. You can view any ClojureScript program as a collection of functions, and interpret its structure by observing the function call graph.

However, with only a very slight shift in viewpoint, you can also understand any functional program in terms of the *data* that it manipulates and how that data flows through the system. Every function takes some data as arguments and returns data when it is complete. Usually, the end *goal* of a program is not to invoke certain execution paths, but to create, retrieve, or transform data in one form or another. Functions are simply the tool for doing so. In a very real sense, one could say that "data-oriented programing" is a synonym for "functional programming."

Clojure and ClojureScript recognize this, and therefore provide a carefully-designed set of data primitives and composite data structures that are both easy to use and philosophically aligned with basic theories about what data *is*. It is a common remark among experienced Clojure programmers that they came to Clojure for the concurrency, but stayed for the data structures. ClojureScript brings these data structures and their associated mindset to the browser, where they have proven to be an equally good fit.

Primitives

ClojureScript provides a small set of primitive data types. Each type maps directly to one of JavaScript's native types. As in JavaScript, all of ClojureScript's primitives are *immutable*, meaning that each is a value unto itself and cannot be changed. Immutability is an important feature of ClojureScript, and will be discussed in much greater detail later on.

Strings

Strings represent textual data, as a sequence of characters. They can be entered as literals in a ClojureScript program using double quotes. Although they are primitives, it is also possible to obtain a *sequence* view of a string as a sequence of characters (see the next chapter).

Under the hood, ClojureScript strings are JavaScript strings, and may be freely passed to (or received from) JavaScript functions and libraries that expect (or return) strings.

Keywords

Keywords are very similar to strings in that they are sequences of characters. Actually, in ClojureScript, they are nearly identical to strings except for their intended use. Typically keywords are used as keys in maps, for constants, or for enumerated sets of values. As a rule of thumb, it is idiomatic to use a keyword wherever the value is of interest to the program or programmer, rather than data for the user.

In Clojure, keywords are guaranteed to be *interned* (that is, all instances of the same keyword will always refer to the same object in memory, making them very efficient). This is not the case in ClojureScript, since at the JavaScript level keywords are implemented as plain old JavaScript strings. Still, it is good practice to create keywords only for a constrained, finite set of values.

Keywords may optionally be *namespace qualified*, meaning that they have a separate namespace component to them, and are logically associated with a particular namespace (namespaces are discussed in Chapter 7). To create a namespace-qualified keyword as a literal, include a slash in the keyword. For example, :my-ns/foo creates a keyword with a name of "foo" in a namespace called "my-ns." You can also use a double leading colon to create a namespace-qualified keyword in the current namespace (e.g., ::foo).

Keywords also support some additional operations; for example, they can be used as functions that know how to look themselves up in maps, which we will see later.

Symbols

Symbols are also very similar to strings, and like keywords, they can be namespace-qualified. In ClojureScript they are used almost exclusively as named bindings (i.e., "variable" names, even though ClojureScript doesn't really have variables as such). The literal form of a symbol is simply the raw text (foo), with a slash if it is namespace-qualified (foo/bar).

There is typically no reason to create or use symbols as data in your program, unless you're working with macros (discussed in Chapter 8). Although they're a key part of the data that represents your program itself (remember, Lisp code is data), keywords or strings are usually better choices for the data your program actually manipulates.

In ClojureScript, symbols are also implemented as JavaScript strings.

Characters

Characters are a single textual character, and can be expressed as literals with a leading backslash (e.g., \a for the character "a").

Since JavaScript doesn't have a native character type, ClojureScript characters are implemented as single-character strings, and behave identically to strings.

Numbers

ClojureScript's numbers are the same as JavaScript numerics and can be either integers or floating-point numbers. They are expressed literally as numerals (for example, 42 or 3.14). Conversions and coercions between integer and floating point happen automatically; ClojureScript has the same arithmetic semantics as JavaScript.

You can pass a ClojureScript numeric value to any JavaScript function that expects a numeric, and receive them the same way.

Unlike Clojure, ClojureScript does not currently support additional numeric types such as Ratio, BigDecimal, or BigInteger.

Booleans

Boolean values are always one of two values, true or false, representing logical truth and falsehood, respectively. ClojureScript Booleans, like strings and numerics, are implemented directly as JavaScript Boolean values and may be used accordingly in interop scenarios.

> Note that although the basic *values* for Boolean true and false are the same in ClojureScript and JavaScript, the semantics of what constitutes truth can be different. For example, the number zero, when used in a Boolean expression, is false in JavaScript but true in ClojureScript. See the sidebar on "Truthiness" in Chapter 4.

To use a Boolean as a literal, just type one of the special symbols true or false.

Functions

In ClojureScript (like JavaScript), functions are first-class entities and, as befits a functional programming language, are themselves data. They can be created using the syntax discussed in the previous chapter, and once created can be passed around and added to composite data structures like any other data.

Importantly, ClojureScript functions are implemented as plain old JavaScript functions. This means that they can be passed to any JavaScript library that takes a function as a callback (for example), and given a JavaScript function, you can invoke it using ClojureScript syntax. (Unless, of course, the JavaScript function contains a reference to this. Internally, ClojureScript always invokes functions using their call method and passes in nil as the value for this.)

nil

ClojureScript's nil is identical to null in JavaScript; it is used where a value is logically absent, empty, or meaningless. To use it as a literal, just use the special symbol nil. ClojureScript does not use JavaScript's undefined value, but you can refer to it as js/undefined.

Table 5-1. Quick reference for primitive data types

ClojureScript type	literal	example(s)	JS type
string	double quotes	"string"	string
symbol	plain characters	symbol	string
keyword	leading colon	:keyword	string
character	leading backslash	\c	string
number	literal number	42, 3.14	numeric
boolean	'true' or 'false'	true, false	boolean
function	(fn ...) or #(...)	#(* 2 %)	function
nil	'nil'	nil	null

Data Structures

ClojureScript also provides a full complement of composite collection types. These collections can contain ClojureScript's primitive types or other collections, as well as any other object that JavaScript itself supports. However, using non-ClojureScript objects as values in ClojureScript collections may invalidate some of the guarantees ClojureScript can make regarding equality semantics and serializability.

ClojureScript collections that contain only primitives or other ClojureScript collections *do* make certain guarantees:

Equality

Collections with the same semantics containing the same values are considered equal for all purposes, even if they are different instances in the JavaScript VM. ClojureScript equality is always value-dependent, and the value of a collection is defined in terms of its contents. Note that this is true even across implementations, as long as the semantics of the collection are the same. For example, a map can only be equal to another map, but that map may be any of the alternative map implementations (see the section on maps below).

Serializability

Obtaining the string value of a collection always results in a string that, when read back using the ClojureScript reader, will be equal to the original. This is extremely useful for simple cases of storing and transmitting data.

Clojure compatibility

The serialized string representation of ClojureScript objects and collections is fully compatible with that of Clojure. Objects printed in ClojureScript can be read in Clojure, and vice versa. This makes development Clojure on the server side and ClojureScript in the browser client very easy. We will demonstrate this technique in Chapter 10.

JSON and ClojureScript

Because ClojureScript has such good string serialization for its own object types, using JSON in a ClojureScript program is not encouraged unless needed to interact with a third-party or legacy API. Just as JSON stands for "JavaScript Object Notation" and is useful precisely because it matches JavaScript's syntax, Clojure's collection literal strings can be thought of as "Clojure Collection Notation" and match ClojureScript's syntax and semantics, with baked-in language support. Therefore, they are usually more suitable for the Clojure and ClojureScript environment. However, JSON parsers and serializers are still available via the Google Closure Library or built-in browser functions.

Efforts are underway to create a formal specification for Clojure/ClojureScript data under the name "Extensible Data Notation." Details are at *https://github.com/edn-format/edn*.

Collection Types

Lists

Lists are ordered collections of items, implemented as singly-linked lists. As such, they support fast lookups and insertions at the head of the list and $O(n)$ reads in the general case.

The literal syntax for writing lists is simply parentheses around the items (e.g., (1 2 3)). However, lists are also used in ClojureScript code to indicate a form that should be evaluated, meaning that if you try to enter a list that you *don't* want evaluated (such as the one above), you'll get an error as it tries to execute something it shouldn't.

To avoid this and create a list literal, you can *quote* the form using either the quote special form or the single quote reader macro, which prevent evaluation of the forms to which they are applied. They are completely equivalent: '(1 2 3) is identical to (quote (1 2 3)), and both will evaluate to a list consisting of the numbers 1, 2, and 3 without attempting to evaluate 1 as a function.

To prepend an item to a list, use the conj function, which takes a collection as its first argument and any number of additional items to add. The items will be added at the beginning of the list. To retrieve items from a list, use the sequence functions (described in "Vectors").

Vectors

Vectors are also ordered collections of items, and should generally be preferred to lists in most ClojureScript code. They fill the role played by arrays in JavaScript and most other programming languages, having near-constant lookup, update, and append operations. Technically, the computational complexity of a vector lookup is $O(log_{32}(n))$, but this is so close to constant time that the distinction is practically meaningless on any data structure that will fit in memory on a modern computer.

The literal syntax for a vector is square brackets surrounding the items, such as [1 2 3] or [:a :b :c]. You've already seen literal vectors: they are used for specifying function parameters.

To append an item to a vector, use the conj function as you would for a list. However, in the case of a vector, the item(s) will be appended rather than prepended (conj works differently depending on the type of collection).

You can retrieve items from a vector using the sequence functions. The nth function will efficiently retrieve the item at a particular index. Vectors themselves can also be invoked as functions, passing an integer as the argument will return the item stored at that index (e.g., ([:a :b :c] 1) returns :b). To return a vector with an updated value at a particular index, use the assoc function (which takes a vector, an index, and a value) and returns a vector with the update applied.

Maps

Maps are associative collections; that is, they associate keys with values, and allow efficient retrieval of a value by its key. They are similar to Hashes in Ruby, HashTables in Java, or associative arrays (i.e., objects) in JavaScript.

The literal syntax for a map is alternating key/value pairs surrounded by curly braces, such as {:key1 :val1 :key2 :val2}. Because commas are whitespace in ClojureScript, some people like to add them to maps for greater visual distinction between key/value pairs like {:k1 :v1, :k2 :v2}, but this is strictly optional.

Note that keys can be any primitive or data type that supports proper equality. Keywords are idiomatic and efficient, but strings and integers are also commonly used as map keys. It is even perfectly acceptable to use other data structures as keys if they support good equality semantics (as ClojureScript's do).

Maps may actually be implemented in a number of different ways, using different algorithms. ClojureScript includes array maps (backed by arrays), hash maps (backed by hash tables), and tree maps (backed by red-black balanced binary search trees). There are no semantic differences between these implementations, although they do have different performance characteristics. (The sorted tree map does actually make one additional guarantee that other implementations don't: when iterating over its entry set, the entries will be returned in the specified sort order of the keys.) Typically, however, you don't need to worry about them. When you create a map using a literal, ClojureScript chooses the best algorithm based on the size of the map, and will swap out the type to keep it efficient as it grows. If you wish, however, you can create a particular type of map using the `array-map`, `hash-map`, or `sorted-map/sorted-map-by` functions (for array maps, hash maps, and tree maps, respectively).

There are several techniques for retrieving values from a map:

- The `get` function, which takes a map and a key value, and returns the value mapped to the key.
- The map itself can be invoked as a function. Passing it a key will return the value mapped to that key.
- If the key is a keyword, you can invoke it as a function, passing the map as an argument. When used as a function, keywords can look themselves up in the map they are provided and return the associated value.

To obtain a map with an inserted or updated value at a particular field, use the `assoc` function, passing a map and a series of alternating keys and values. This will return the map, but with the specified keys mapped to the specified values. If the map previously contained values associated with the keys, they will be replaced.

Sets

Sets are unordered collections of unique items, meaning that the same item cannot be duplicated in the set (similar to the mathematical notion of a set). If you add an item to a set that is equal to an item the set already contains, the set is unaffected. Sets can also be thought of as maps with only keys and no values. They support fast insertion, removal, and membership checks.

The literal syntax for a set is a pound sign followed by members enclosed in curly braces, like `#{:a :b :c}`.

To add an item to a set, use the `conj` function, passing the set and the item to add. Sets also support `disj`, which does the opposite of `conj` and returns a set with the item removed. To test if an item is a member of a set, use the `contains?` function, which takes a set and an item and returns true if the item is a member of the set.

ClojureScript also provides the `clojure.set` namespace containing dedicated set operations such as `union`, `intersection`, and `difference`.

Immutability

An important feature of all of ClojureScript's collections is that they are *immutable*, meaning that they can't be changed. Functions that "modify" collections don't actually ever change them, but instead create and return a new one based on the original with the specified differences in place.

This is highly nonintuitive to most programmers who don't have prior experience with purely functional languages. However, it becomes clearer once you understand Clojure(Script)'s concept of *value*.

Values don't change. Consider the number 3. If you add 3 + 1, you haven't *changed* the value of 3 (which would wreak havoc with math and physics everywhere). Instead, you've acquired a *new* value. The same is true of words: if you use the word "good" together with the word "morning" to say "good morning," you haven't changed the global meaning of the word "good," you've used it to create a new utterance. In ClojureScript, the very *definition* of a value means that it can't change—if it does, it's no longer the same value.

ClojureScript's collections are all values. If I take the vector [1 2] and append the value 4, I haven't changed the meaning of [1 2]. I *can't* change it. By definition, it can only ever mean "the two element vector consisting of the integers 1 and 2." If I could literally change it, it would no longer meet its own definition. But what I *can* do is create an entirely new vector, using [1 2] as a base: [1 2 4].

The same thing is true of all ClojureScript's other collection types. When you add a member to a set, you're creating a different set with different members (which, incidentally, conforms to the mathematical definition of a set). When you add an item to the front of a list, you create a new list consisting of both the old list and the new item. When you add a new key to a map, you're creating a new map, with a different set of keys.

Why immutability?

In Clojure, concurrency is always listed as a compelling reason to use immutable collections: preventing unexpected changes to data goes a long way towards preventing race conditions. HTML 5 WebWorkers do allow concurrent execution in modern browsers. However, they sidestep many of the difficulties associated with concurrent programming by forbidding shared state between threads, instead operating solely on the basis of message passing. But what about ClojureScript, which always runs in a single-threaded JavaScript environment?

There are two possible answers to this question. First, there is a sense in which treating collections as values is philosophically *correct*, irrespective of performance or design implications. It makes programs easier to formalize and reason about. For example, having a firm concept of collections as values also allows a rigorous notion of equality (which can greatly simplify programs), and allows functions dealing with collections to remain formally pure.

Second, there are indeed practical benefits to having immutable objects besides full concurrency. Even though JavaScript is single-threaded, code is often structured in terms of asynchronous callbacks and event loops, and it isn't always easy to reconstruct the exact sequence of execution a program might take. With immutable values, you can rely on the fact that once you have obtained a collection, you can save it (either explicitly or by closing over it) and use it later without any risk that it will have changed. Having immutable objects means never having to worry about mentally keeping track of what's going on—all value changes are explicit and apparent in the code.

Persistence

One question that almost invariably follows a discussion of immutability is that of the performance implications. No matter what the benefits are, isn't cloning an entire data structure every time it's updated prohibitively wasteful of computational resources?

The answer would be yes, if that were what actually happens. Fortunately, ClojureScript provides some extremely sophisticated data structure implementations that utilize the concept of *persistence* to provide objects that are logically immutable, but share structure with previous versions of themselves to minimize their computational overhead.

A full discussion of the implementation of persistent data structures is beyond the scope of this book, but essentially what happens is that when a data structure is modified, the new value is not a full clone of the original one. Instead, it incorporates the original (which it can safely do, because the old one is immutable) plus the changes, and then exposes a unified view of the whole package in a way that hides the internal structure.

In practical terms, persistence means that while using immutable objects does incur some small overhead compared with mutating traditional objects, it (hopefully) falls well within the realm of acceptable cost relative to the benefit provided. Typically, unless you're writing extremely performance-sensitive code (which is rare in JavaScript to begin with), ClojureScript's immutable collections are more than fast enough. And if you ever do need to eke out every last drop of performance, ClojureScript's interop syntax makes it easy to drop down to native JavaScript objects and arrays.

Identity and State

Having data structures be immutable values is all very well, but it opens another question: if values are immutable, then how does ClojureScript model state and change over time? After all, not every program can be a purely functional transformation of inputs to outputs. Most of the time, programs need to store and change values.

The answer lies in ClojureScript's (and Clojure's) conceptual distinctions among value, identity, and state.

- A value is, as the name implies, an immutable value. As discussed above, values can't change, by definition.
- Identity refers to a named entity in the system that may refer to different values at different points in time.
- State refers to the value of an identity at a particular point in time.

Most languages don't make a clear distinction between these concepts—for example, a variable in JavaScript has bits of all three. It is a named thing, but it has a value, and its value can change.

By teasing apart these concepts, ClojureScript makes state management *explicit*. Identities are clearly visible as the only things that can change, and state transitions to new values are clearly intentional.

This leads to a unique program structure in large ClojureScript programs. Rather than having state smeared thinly across the whole program, it is isolated from the main bulk of the code. Only a few functions update state, the rest remain pure functions of values. When done correctly, this makes ClojureScript programs *much* easier to reason about than those written in object-oriented or imperative paradigms.

Atoms

In Clojure, there are several constructs for creating identities, including atoms, refs, and agents. The different types of identities differ in the concurrency semantics they support. In ClojureScript, which doesn't need to support shared-memory concurrency, there is only one type: atoms.

Atoms are identities that refer to a single value (though that value, of course, may be one of Clojure's collections). All updates to the state of an atom are *atomic*, that is, they occur in a single operation.

To create an atom, just use the `atom` function, passing a value for the initial state. For example:

```
(def my-atom (atom {}))
```

This constructs an atom with an initial state of an empty map, and binds it to a var called my-atom.

To retrieve the current value of an atom, use the deref function, which also has a shortened syntax using the reader macro @. The following two expressions are equivalent:

```
(deref my-atom)   ;=> {}
@my-atom   ;=> {}
```

There are two ways to update the state of an atom, swap! and reset!. swap! is used to update the atom's state in terms of the previous state, reset! sets the state without regard for the previous state. Both functions return the value of the atom's new state.

swap! always takes at least two arguments; the first is the atom, the second is the update function. The update function will be applied with the value of the atom as its first argument, with any additional arguments to swap! used as additional arguments.

So, for example, to add a new entry to the map that is the current value of my-atom, you could invoke swap! like so:

```
(swap! my-atom assoc :a "1")   ;=> {:a 1}
```

Subsequently, retrieving the value of the atom returns the new value:

```
@my-atom   ;=> {:a 1}
```

Or, you can use reset!, passing the atom and the new value to update the state:

```
(reset! my-atom {:x 42})   ;=> {:x 42}
@my-atom   ;=> {:x 42}
```

Initially, this might seem like too much ceremony to do something as easy as changing some state. But the ceremony is (almost) the whole point. State should *not* be something implicit in a program, quietly multiplying complexity exponentially with each new variable. Instead, it should be carefully, knowingly managed. In ClojureScript, atoms provide this capability.

CHAPTER 6

Sequences

One of the key features of the Lisp family of languages is their orientation around lists —not just as data structures, but as a structural metaphor for algorithms and execution flow. Recursive algorithms, for example, can be very cleanly structured around lists in Lisp variants.

Unfortunately, in most Lisps, this metaphor is tightly bound to the actual implementation of a singly-linked list, which has performance characteristics that make it unsuitable for many purposes.

To resolve this problem, Clojure introduced a new abstraction around the concept of a list, called a *sequence*, which is shared by ClojureScript. A sequence is a logical list, similar to those in most Lisps, with a well-defined set of operations. However, Clojure sequences are not a concrete type, but rather an abstract contract that may be satisfied concretely by a variety of different types of objects. All of ClojureScript's collections, as well as many other types of logical collections in JavaScript, can be used as sequences. This allows ClojureScript code to be constructed in an idiomatic list-based Lisp style, while using whatever data structure is actually most appropriate for the job.

Many common operations in ClojureScript are part of the *sequence API*. Functions from the sequence API are used to select items from sequences, add items to sequences, and produce, consume, and transform sequences. Understanding how sequences work will give you a major leg up in understanding and writing idiomatic ClojureScript code and, once you get the hang of it, will help you write functions of your own that are highly general and composable with other sequence functions.

The Sequence Abstraction

The basic definition of a sequence is very simple. All sequences have two elements: a *first*, which is the first element, and a *rest*, a sequence of the remaining elements. An empty *first* and *rest* in ClojureScript are directly analogous to the *car* and *cdr* of older Lisps. They are renamed to be clearer and to emphasize that they are abstract concepts, not inherently bound to any particular implementation of a sequence. A *nil rest* signals the end of the sequence. You can obtain the first or rest of a sequence by using the `first` or `rest` functions.

Anything that can be represented as a first and a rest can be a sequence. The `seq` function is used to polymorphically obtain a sequence view of any object that supports it. Calling `seq` explicitly to convert a collection is rarely necessary, however, since sequence functions (including `first` and `rest`) call `seq` on their argument for you.

Lists and vectors are the most obvious sequences, being naturally ordered collections of elements:

```
(first [:a :b :c])  ;=> :a
(rest [:a :b :c])   ;=> (:b :c)

(first '(1 2 3))    ;=> 1
(rest '(1 2 3))     ;=> (2 3)
```

Sets are also sequences. Although they are unordered, you can still use sequence functions on them; the elements will just be cast into an arbitrary (though consistent, for the same set) order:

```
(first #{:b :c :a})  ;=> :a
(rest #{:b :c :a})   ;=> (:b :c)
```

Maps are also sequences of key-value pairs, represented as two-element vectors and returned in arbitrary order:

```
(first {:b 2 :a 1 :c 3})  ;=> [:a 1]
(rest {:b 2 :a 1 :c 3})   ;=> ([:c 3] [:b 2])
```

Other items which can be viewed as a sequence (*sequable* objects) include native Java-Script arrays and strings (as sequences of their constituent characters).

Lazy Sequences

Despite their obvious utility for working with data structures, one of the advantages of sequences is that they don't *need* to be backed by an actual data structure in memory. All they have to do is implement `first` and `rest` meaningfully.

This leads to an interesting and extremely useful feature: it is possible to have sequences with a rest that isn't actually created until you call the `rest` function. Sequences with a nonrealized rest are known as *lazy sequences*. Because lazy sequences don't have to fully exist in memory all at once, they can be arbitrarily large, even infinite.

For example, in ClojureScript, it is possible to construct an infinite sequence of every positive integer using the `iterate` function:

```
(do
  (def i (iterate inc 0))
  nil)
```

As an aside, note that the `def` is wrapped in a `do`, which returns `nil`. This is only to prevent the value of the `i` symbol from being printed back at the REPL, which ClojureScript does by default. `i` can exist as a lazy sequence using hardly any memory, but if you try to print it, it will try to print the entire thing to the REPL. Obviously, this is impossible. This is one thing to be careful of when using infinite lazy sequences: don't do something that would cause them to be printed! This will almost certainly crash your process and force you to restart.

`iterate` is a higher-order function that takes two arguments, a function and an initial value. It returns a lazy sequence with a first element of the initial value. Its rest sequence is lazily constructed, and in turn has an first value of the function applied to the initial value. Its rest, also lazy, is the result of applying the function to the previous value, and so on.

So, by starting with the `inc` function and an initial value of `0`, the above expression constructs a sequence where each successive element is constructed by incrementing the previous element; this is a sequence of the positive integers. But the calculation is only performed when the sequence is actually realized, so it doesn't end up using an infinite amount of memory.

Letting Go of the Head

Lazy sequences are cached, so each element is realized only once, and then stored instead of being recalculated. This means that expensive computations won't be run unnecessarily. It also means that it's safe to have sequence generating functions with side effects —they may not happen at all, if the sequence is never realized, but they'll never be executed repeatedly.

The downside is that lazy sequences *do* consume memory, once they've been realized. For this reason, if you're processing a very large or infinite sequence, it's important not to maintain a reference to the head of the sequence as you iterate over it. That way, the earlier parts of the sequence can be garbage collected each time you move forward on the sequence. But if you maintain a reference to the entire sequence, its elements will be cached, not garbage collected, and you're likely to get out-of-memory errors.

The Sequence API

ClojureScript has a large library of functions that operate on sequences. Although you don't have to know them all, familiarity with the basic ones covered here is critical to writing idiomatic functional code. In particular, you should become very comfortable with map, reduce, and filter if you're not already; these are the staples of the functional programming style.

map

map is a higher order function that takes a function (which takes a single argument) and a sequence, and returns a sequence of items resulting from applying the function to each item in the input sequence. It is lazy; the input sequence is only consumed and the mapping function applied when the resulting sequence is realized. As such, it can be used on an infinite sequence to return a new infinite sequence.

For example, the following expression applies a function to obtain the square of every number in the input sequence:

```
(map (fn [n] (* n n)) [1 2 3 4 5])  ;=> (1 4 9 16 25)
```

map can also take more than one sequence. In this case, the function provided must take the same number of arguments as there are sequences, and the function is applied to the first member of each sequence, then the second, third, and so on. Processing stops at the end of the shortest sequence. For example:

```
(map (fn [a b] (+ a b)) [1 2 3] [10 20 30 40])  ;=> (11, 22, 33)
```

reduce

reduce is a function that takes a function and a sequence and uses the provided function to consume the entire sequence and return a single value. As such, it is not lazy and should not be used on infinite sequences.

The supplied function must take two arguments; it is first invoked on the first two elements of the sequence, then invoked again with the resulting value and the third item, then with the result of *that* and the fourth item, and so on until the sequence is consumed.

The following example uses the + function to obtain a sum of the numbers in a sequence:

```
(reduce + [1 2 3 4])  ;=> 10
```

You can also invoke reduce with three arguments, supplying an initial value as the second argument to reduce. It will be used along with the first element from the sequence in the first function invocation, instead of using the first two values from the sequence.

filter

filter takes a function and a sequence, and returns a sequence consisting only of the items for which applying the function to items in the input sequence returns logical true. It is fully lazy, although consuming a single item in the resulting sequence may "jump" forward in the input sequence until it finds one that meets the specified criteria.

The following example uses the built-in integer? function to return a filtered sequence only of numbers that are integers:

```
(filter integer? [1 2.71 3.14 5 42])  ;=> (1 5 42)
```

Other Useful Sequence Functions

Although there are a great many other sequence functions you'll want to explore, here are some of the most frequently used:

cons
> Takes an item and a sequence, and returns a new sequence with the item as its first and the sequence as its rest.

count
> Takes a sequence as its argument, and returns the length of a sequence. It must realize the entire sequence to do so, so don't call it on an infinite sequence as it will never return.

nth
> Takes a sequence and an index (starting from zero), and returns the item at that location in the sequence. For example, (nth x 5) returns the *sixth* item in x.

take
> Takes a number n and a sequence, and returns a new sequence consisting of the first n items in the input sequence. It is fully lazy; it will only realize the input sequence when and if the returned sequence is realized.

drop
> Takes a number n and a sequence, and returns a new sequence of all the items in the input sequence *except* for the first n items. It is also lazy.

concat
> Takes any number of sequences as arguments, and returns a single sequence containing all the items in each of the input sequences. It is lazy.

reverse
> Takes a single sequence and returns a sequence of its items in reverse order. It cannot be lazy, since it needs to realize the entire input sequence in order to get its last item.

Finally, there is a special sequence generator that's actually a macro, not a function:

lazy-seq

This is the basic, low-level way to create lazy sequences. It is a macro that takes any number of forms as its body. The body, when evaluated, should return a sequence or `nil`. However, the body isn't evaluated right away. Instead, it's stored in a closure, and `lazy-seq` returns an *unrealized* lazy sequence. Only if the sequence is eventually realized will the body be invoked, returning the result of the body as the realized sequence.

By making recursive function calls in the body of `lazy-seq`, it's possible to construct lazy sequences of arbitrary or infinite length.

Normally, it's not necessary to use `lazy-seq` directly; usually, one of the provided sequence-generating functions is more suitable. `iterate`, in particular, is very flexible. However, when you need it, `lazy-seq` can be a powerful tool to create arbitrary lazy sequences.

CHAPTER 7

Namespaces, Libraries, and Google Closure

So far, we've talked mostly about basic features of the language such as syntax, semantics, and the compilation process. ClojureScript also offers compelling features at a higher structural level to facilitate code organization and sharing libraries.

In ClojureScript, as in Clojure, the highest level of code organization is namespaces, used to scope global definitions. However, despite superficial similarities, namespaces in ClojureScript are implemented completely differently than they are in Clojure because it runs in a different environment. This chapter will cover what these differences are and how to use namespaces effectively in ClojureScript.

Additionally, this chapter will describe how to create and utilize libraries. Unfortunately, one of the negative effects of ClojureScript's reliance on the Google Closure Compiler is the fact that creating and consuming libraries is not always straightforward, particularly in light of Google Closure's *Advanced Optimizations* mode.

Namespaces

To avoid name collisions, ClojureScript symbols and keywords have a namespace component. Each *.cljs* file has its own namespace, and every REPL session has a *current* namespace (cljs.user by default). Whenever you define a symbol using def or one of its derivatives (such as defn), the namespace of the symbol is set to the current namespace. Symbols with the same name in different namespaces are completely different, and will not clash.

In addition to name disambiguation, namespaces are also ClojureScript's unit of code dependency management. A namespace may *require* or *use* other namespaces as dependencies, and dependent namespaces are always loaded before the namespace that required them when the program is run. ClojureScript does not support circular references between namespaces.

One very important difference between namespaces in ClojureScript and Clojure is that while Clojure namespaces are first-class entities that can be dynamically created and loaded at runtime, ClojureScript namespaces are statically resolved at *compile time only*. You can't create or load a namespace during program execution.

Using Namespaces

As you have already seen, if you refer to a symbol without specifying a namespace, ClojureScript will attempt to resolve the symbol in the current namespace. To specify a namespace, use a slash between the namespace and the name. For example, `foo.bar/hello` references a symbol named `hello` in the `foo.bar` namespace, which is distinct from a symbol named `hello` in any other namespace.

To specify a namespace for a source file, use the `ns` special form as the first form in the file. (Unlike Clojure, `ns` is not just a macro wrapping more primitive functions (such as `load` and `require`) but built in to the language directly.) In its most basic form, declaring a namespace called `foo.bar` looks like this:

```
(ns foo.bar)
```

In ClojureScript, as in Clojure, the namespace of a file needs to match its location on the Java classpath. In the case of ClojureScript, this is the classpath of the compiler. Each . (period or full stop) in the namespace translates to a subdirectory on the classpath. For example, the namespace `foo.bar.baz` should be in a file with the path `foo/bar/baz.cljs`, relative to the classpath. This is necessary for the ClojureScript compiler to find the file that corresponds to a namespace.

To specify that a namespace depends on another namespace, add a `:require` form in the `ns` form, containing any number of specifications:

```
(ns application
    (:require [foo.bar :as bar]
              [foo.baz :as baz]))
```

This will force loading of the `foo.bar` and `foo.baz` namespaces before `application` itself is loaded. Labeling the namespaces with the `:as` clause means that within the foo namespace, you can reference the symbols in `foo.bar` via a shorter "alias" `bar`. In this example, the symbol `foo.bar/function` can be written `bar/function`. ClojureScript, unlike Clojure, does not permit "bare" namespaces in a `:require` clause. The compiler will throw an exception if you specify a `:require` without `:as`.

You may also reference namespaces with `:use` instead of `:require`, like so:

```
(ns application
    (:use [foo.bar :only [hello goodbye]]))
```

The `:use` form also causes the specified namespace(s) to be loaded, but differs from `:require` in that, for each of the symbols specified in the `:only` vector, it establishes a synonym in the current namespace so you can refer to symbols in the used namespace without explicitly qualifying them. For example, given the above ns declaration, you can now use the symbols hello and goodbye directly in the foo namespace to refer to foo.bar/hello and foo.bar/goodbye.

Again, the use of :only in a :use specification is mandatory in ClojureScript, and will cause a compile error if missing. Additionally, unlike Clojure, :require and :use are the only forms allowed within an ns declaration. Clojure's :import, :refer, etc., are not supported. Therefore, although a valid ClojureScript ns declaration is also always a valid Clojure ns declaration, the inverse is not true: ClojureScript has much narrower requirements for validity.

Using namespaces at the REPL

The ns form will not work in the ClojureScript REPL (either the Rhino REPL or the browser REPL). To switch the current namespace in the REPL, you can use the in-ns special form, passing it the quoted namespace:

```
ClojureScript:cljs.user> (in-ns 'foo.bar)
```

This switches the REPL's current namespace to be foo.bar.

Note that in-ns is a special tool for REPL development, and doesn't actually exist in ClojureScript's standard library. It is implemented as a special case in the REPL's reader. As such, it won't work at all in *.cljs* source files, or anywhere else except in a REPL session.

Also, because ClojureScript namespaces can be defined only at compile time, using in-ns to switch to a namespace does not implicitly create the namespace (as it does in Clojure). If you specify a namespace that isn't already loaded, the REPL will switch to it, but almost everything you try to do will fail with a "namespace is not defined" error.

Using Namespaces Effectively

Fundamentally, namespaces are just a tool to prevent name clashes, but they also help structure your code into logical units. They function a bit like modules or packages in other languages. Here are a few hints to use namespaces effectively:

1. Group similar or related functions together in the same namespace.
2. Try to minimize the number of dependencies (:require and :use expressions) in each namespace, except for one main namespace that ties together everything in your application.
3. Never have circular dependencies between two namespaces (namespace *A* depends on *B*, which depends on *A*).

The Implementation of Namespaces

To really understand how ClojureScript namespaces work, it's helpful to know something about their implementation.

Namespaces and *.js files

When you compile a directory containing *.cljs files, the compiler emits a directory with the same structure containing compiled *.js files; each input *.cljs file has exactly one output *.js file with the same name and path.

Each emitted *.js file contains code allowing it to participate in the namespace system provided by the Google Closure Library. You can read about the Google Closure Library's dependency management system here (*https://developers.google.com/closure/library/*). Note that as a user of ClojureScript, you don't have to worry about writing a *deps.js* file, or using the ClojureBuilder or DepsWriter scripts described in the Google Closure documentation. The ClojureScript compiler performs those functions internally. This is the mechanism by which ClojureScript actually resolves namespace dependencies: under the hood, ClojureScript's namespace dependency system *is* that of Google Closure.

In the Google Closure Library, dependency management is handled by two functions: goog.provide() and goog.require(). The goog.provide() function is intended to be called once per file, and passes the namespace the file contains. The goog.require() function may be called multiple times, each time with a dependency of the file. Both are emitted directly by ClojureScript when compiling an ns form. The mapping is very straightforward:

```
(ns application
    (:require [foo.bar :as bar]
              [foo.baz :as baz]))
```

It is compiled to:

```
goog.provide("application");
goog.require("foo.bar");
goog.require("foo.baz");
```

What happens next depends on what :optimizations mode the ClojureScript compiler is running in.

When using :optimizations :none, the ClojureScript compiler will write a list of calls to goog.addDependency() to the specified :output-to file. These serve to create mappings between namespace names, dependencies, and relative paths, and are necessary to inform Google Closure of the location of dependencies (unlike ClojureScript, Google Closure has no convention regarding source file location). After you include this dependencies file in your web page, calls to goog.require() will dynamically add new <script> tags to the page using the provided relative path.

It follows, then, that when using :optimizations :none you must also make the compiler output directory (specified with :output-dir) publicly available on a relative path appropriate to the URL of the page. This is necessary because the page will end up loading each of the needed *.js files directly. You must also manually include goog/base.js first in your HTML, to bootstrap the Google Closure Library, as we showed in Chapter 3.

On the other hand, when using any :optimizations mode *other* than :none, the compiler will concatenate all the required files into one gigantic JavaScript file, in dependency order, and write it out as the :output-to file. This is the only *.js file you need to include on your HTML page, since it contains a full copy of every dependency, even the core Google Closure library. Therefore, in this case, it *isn't* necessary to expose the output directory like it is with :optimizations :none.

Namespaces and variable names

Because vanilla JavaScript has no built-in namespace support, it's standard practice to use objects as a poor man's namespace system, nesting all the variables a library uses under a single top-level object.

The ClojureScript compiler does exactly the same thing, when compiling ClojureScript symbols to JavaScript variables. Each dot-separated level of the namespace becomes a nested object, with the symbol's name as the final name. For example, the symbol my.cool.new-project/some-data in ClojureScript will be my.cool.new_project. some_data in JavaScript. (Hyphens in ClojureScript symbols become underscores in JavaScript.)

For pure ClojureScript applications, this is just an implementation detail. However, it does become important when you want to call a ClojureScript function from JavaScript, since you must refer to it by its fully qualified (i.e., nested) name.

Advanced Compilation Mode

For the subsequent sections on consuming and producing libraries, one of the major challenges is working with the implications of the Google Closure Compiler's *Advanced Optimizations* mode. Before moving on, it will help to have a complete idea of what *Advanced* mode actually does.

Advanced mode's blessing, and its curse, is that it deeply and radically transforms your program. It does so in very beneficial ways, decreasing both code size and execution time, sometimes drastically. *Advanced* mode can and does:

- Rename variables and functions to shorter names (sometimes called *munging*)
- Flatten object nesting
- Eliminate unused code

- Create inline functions
- Optimize performance based on known characteristics of JavaScript runtimes

Essentially, there is nothing that advanced mode might not do to your code, while maintaining the same semantics. Consider the following example:

```
function print_sum(sum) {
    alert('The sum is ' + sum);
}
print_sum(3 + 4);
```

Advanced mode can convert this to the following:

```
alert("The sum is 7");
```

The level of sophistication evident in this transformation speaks for itself.

But *Advanced* mode's power comes at a price. Specifically, it imposes two major requirements:

1. It must operate on the entire program, as a whole, at once. Otherwise, it cannot safely rename variables or enact other transformations.

2. It only works on a subset of JavaScript. The exact restrictions can be found here (*https://developers.google.com/closure/compiler/docs/limitations*). You don't have to worry about this for ClojureScript code, since the ClojureScript compiler only emits compatible JavaScript. However, there are frequently issues with third-party libraries not designed with Google Closure in mind.

Consuming Libraries

A compelling feature of ClojureScript is that it is capable of utilizing any JavaScript library. Unfortunately, because of its reliance on Google Closure dependency management and advanced mode compilation, doing so is admittedly difficult. There are several different techniques, and choosing the wrong one will result in errors, or worse, subtle bugs in your application's behavior.

Fortunately, it *is* possible to import and use any library safely, as explained below. See the flowchart at the end of the section for a high-level overview of the options you have.

ClojureScript Libraries

If the library you want to use is written in ClojureScript, your task is done. All you need to do is make sure the **.cljs* files for the library are available on the classpath either as a JAR dependency or a source folder, depending on how the library is distributed.

Once the source files are on the classpath, you can :require or :use them exactly the same way you would a namespace that you wrote—in fact, from the point of view of the system, there isn't any difference. They will be compiled and optimized along with your code.

JavaScript Libraries

You can also use libraries not originally intended for use with ClojureScript by using interop forms in your code to reference JavaScript variables (see Chapter 4).

How exactly to go about including such a library depends on the characteristics of the library in question. The procedure is different for libraries that were written with Google Closure in mind. For those that weren't, there is another choice: compiling them in *Advanced* mode along with your application, or leaving them completely external.

Google Closure libraries

These are files that include a call to goog.provide(), allowing them to participate in Google Clojure's dependency management system, and by extension, ClojureScript's. A JS file that invokes goog.provide('x.y.z') effectively has the namespace x.y.z.

Unless you work at Google, you aren't likely to see many libraries that fit into this category, as Google Closure doesn't have a particularly large uptake in the JavaScript community. However, if you're using a mixed JavaScript/ClojureScript codebase, and you'd like anyone to have the freedom to modify the library, you can consider making your JavaScript compatible with Google Closure to make it easier to use with ClojureScript.

First, to use them, you must start by putting the *.js* files on the classpath so they are accessible to the compiler (just like ClojureScript files).

Second, you must tell the ClojureScript compiler *where* on the classpath the files are located. Unlike ClojureScript file paths, *.js* pathnames don't necessary have any relationship to the namespaces they provide. To indicate this to the compiler, use the :libs compiler option, which is a vector of *.js* pathnames relative to the classpath. The compiler will inspect these files for calls to goog.provide() and handle them appropriately.

For example, to include a library in a file located at jslib/magic.js, the compiler options map might look something like this:

```
{:output-to "resources/public/js/main.js"
 :optimizations :advanced
 :libs ["jslib/magic.js"]}
```

Finally, to use these libraries in your ClojureScript code, :require or :use their namespaces in your ns declaration form. This will ensure that the library is available. Then, use ClojureScript's JS interop to reference the JavaScript vars. Note that the namespace of a Google Closure library doesn't always match the names of the variables it declares; that's another ClojureScript convention that is stricter than what Google Closure alone requires.

Because libraries built for Google Clojure should already be compatible with *Advanced* mode compilation, you shouldn't need to worry about preserving variable names against munging: *Advanced*-mode processing will be consistent across the entire codebase, including the required libraries.

Plain old JavaScript libraries

This is likely the most common type of library you might wish to use in ClojureScript: a normal, possibly popular JavaScript library that wasn't written with ClojureScript or Google Closure in mind.

With these libraries, there is just one major choice to make: do you want to attempt to use the Google Closure Compiler's *Advanced Optimizations* mode to compile the library together with your code, or include it separately on the HTML page? When you use *Advanced* mode, the Google Closure Compiler will perform whole-program optimization across both the library and your code. When you leave it separate, your program will still be compiled, but the external library will be loaded and run without any transformations.

As discussed above, compiling in *Advanced* mode has many benefits in emitted code size and runtime speed. Also, as you will see below, it's slightly easier to use with ClojureScript. However, the fact is that most JavaScript code written without *Advanced* mode in mind probably doesn't meet its rather stringent requirements.

If you *do* want to compile an existing library in *Advanced* mode, you should do a careful audit of the library's code to make sure it meets the restrictions of *Advanced* mode. Be cautious: this is the one area where it is possible to go badly wrong. Sometimes incompatibilities don't manifest in an obvious way until they've caused you serious trouble.

With Advanced mode. Compiling a library into your application with *Advanced* mode is fairly easy, given the major caveat that the library's code is *Advanced*-mode compatible. The process is very similar to including a library that *is* built for Google Closure, the only difference being that instead of just telling the compiler the location of the file, it is necessary to tell it the location and the namespace it provides using the `:foreign-libs` compiler option.

`:foreign-libs` must be a sequence of maps, each containing a `:file` and a `:provides` key. The `:file` value is a path or URL indicating the absolute or classpath-relative location of the file. The `:provides` key is a vector of strings naming the namespaces that the file provides. Put together, it looks like this:

```
{:output-to "resources/public/js/main.js"
 :optimizations :advanced
 :foreign-libs [{:file "http://foo.com/foobar.js"
                 :provides ["foo.bar"]}]}
```

This will tell the ClojureScript compiler that when it's concatenating all the sources prior to running them through the Google Closure Compiler, it should also include the source of the given file, and it should inject a call to `goog.provide()` in the source for each of the given namespaces.

The effect is the same as if the library had included a `goog.provide()` call on its own, and been included using the `:libs` option.

Again, this will only work if the library's code conforms to the standards required by *Advanced* mode. Be especially aware that any nonconformities might not show up at compile time, although Google Closure will do its best to give warnings.

Without Advanced mode. This is likely to be the most common case: you have a library you want to use, but it wasn't built for ClojureScript or Google Clojure, and you're not confident it is compatible with advanced-mode compilation.

The basic premise for using such a library is very simple: just include it on your HTML page using a separate `<script>` tag, which will load it into the JavaScript runtime environment. Since your ClojureScript program has access to the root environment through its interop forms, you can directly reference any of the variables the external library has created using interop forms (such as the `js/` pseudo-namespace).

Unfortunately, although this is fine for *Whitespace Only* or *Simple Optimizations* compilation, *Advanced* mode will cause errors without some extra work. The reason for this is variable munging. *Advanced* mode will potentially rename every symbol or property name mentioned in your ClojureScript code. If you're compiling everything together with *Advanced* mode, the renaming will be consistent and everything will work. But if you're only compiling your ClojureScript code and not the library, then things will be renamed with no way to match them back up, and you'll end up with errors like "X is not a function" or "no such property X" errors.

For a real-world example, consider the following snippet of ClojureScript, which draws a circle using the excellent *Raphael.js* vector graphics library (*http://raphaeljs.com/]* *[http://raphaeljs.com/)*:

```
(let [image (js/Raphael. 10 50 320 200)]
  (.circle image 50 50 50))
```

This works great with *Whitespace Only* or *Simple* compilation. It uses the `js/` namespace to call the global `Raphael` function as a constructor, which creates a Raphael drawing object of the specified dimensions. It then invokes the `circle` method on that object to draw a circle.

But try it in *Advanced* mode, and you'll get a cryptic error, something like new Raphael(10, 50, 320, 200)).K is not a function. Initially, this doesn't make sense: what is the K function it's trying to invoke?

In this case, K is the munged name of circle. Google Closure doesn't know that circle is a name that needs to be preserved. It has no knowledge of the Raphael library at all, since that wasn't included in its compilation pass.

What's needed is a way to inform the Google Closure Compiler that circle is an external reference, and should be left alone when compiling. Fortunately, Google provides such a mechanism: it allows you to create an *externs file*.

An externs file is just a JavaScript file that contains a JavaScript variable and property declarations. Any variable or property referenced in the externs file will not be munged. It isn't actually compiled itself, so the variable references don't have to be meaningful, they just have to be present to signal the compiler not to munge them. A very simple externs file that would make the Raphael code work would be something like this:

```
var Raphael = {};
Raphael.circle = function() {};
```

Of course, Raphael has many more functions than just circle, but you only need to declare the ones you want to consume from ClojureScript.

Finally, you need to tell the ClojureScript compiler about the externs file using the :externs compiler options, which is a sequence of strings of the classpath-relative paths of extern files. For example, to include this externs file for Raphael:

```
{:output-to "resources/public/js/main.js"
 :optimizations :advanced
 :externs ["raphael_externs.js"]}
```

That's it! If you've included the necessary references in an externs file, then you can reference variables and properties from an outside context without munging, and successfully consume any JavaScript library you like.

Creating Libraries

It's fairly straightforward to use ClojureScript to write libraries for distribution and consumption by other applications. You will need to package it differently, however, depending on whether you intend clients of your library to consume it using Clojure-Script or JavaScript (Figure 7-1).

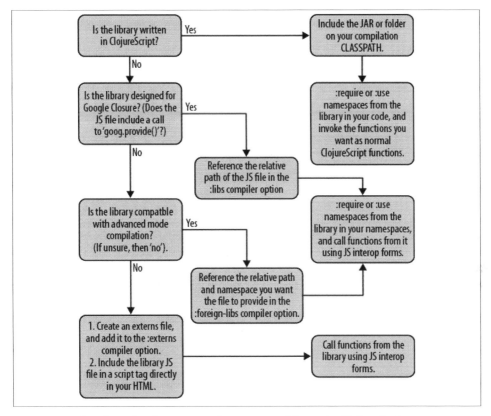

Figure 7-1. Flowchart for determining how to use a library in ClojureScript

For Consumption by ClojureScript

The best way to distribute a ClojureScript library for use by ClojureScript is to distribute the *.cljs* source files directly, either by giving clients a directory full of source code or distributing a JAR file containing the *.cljs* files. In either case, the clients will need to add the directory or JAR to their compiler classpath so the ClojureScript compiler can find them.

All the client has to do to use the library is to consume it as described in the section above on consuming ClojureScript libraries.

For Consumption by JavaScript

If you want JavaScript applications to be able to call your ClojureScript code, you'll need to distribute the *compiled* version of your app. Typically, the easiest way to do this is to compile your library to a single **.js* file using the Google Closure Compiler and give that file to your clients. They can then reference that file in a `<script>` tag on their page, and start using it.

Fortunately, actually using the library should be fairly easy. ClojureScript functions are just JavaScript functions, and namespaces are just nested objects (following the Java-Script convention). So, for example, if you have a ClojureScript function `foo.bar/hello-world`, your JavaScript clients can easily call it using `foo.bar.hello_world()`.

You will have to be careful not to expect arguments or return objects they won't be able to use easily, such as ClojureScript vectors or maps. If you really intend your library to be used extensively from JavaScript, you'll probably want to create a set of public API functions that accept and return more familiar types. For example, you might convert ClojureScript maps to JavaScript objects, sequences to JavaScript arrays, and keywords to strings before returning them.

^:export metadata

If you want to compile your libraries with *Advanced* mode, you'll need to make one small additional change. JavaScript libraries can reference ClojureScript vars by name, but *Advanced* mode compilation munges all the var names. If you want to be able to reference a var from external JavaScript, you'll need to mark it specifically for preservation.

To do this, tag the vars whose names you want to preserve using the `:export` metadata tag. ClojureScript metadata is data that can be attached to any ClojureScript object, and since it can be inspected by the compiler it can be used to alter the emitted JavaScript. In the case of `:export`, it indicates that the tagged var should not be munged.

Adding the `:export` metadata tag to a function using the metadata reader macro looks like this:

```
(ns foo)

(defn ^:export hello [name]
    (js/alert (str "Hello, " name)))
```

This code defines a very simple function called `hello` in the `foo` namespace, but tags it with `:export` so that it won't be munged during advanced compilation. This means that a JavaScript caller can invoke it directly: `foo.hello("Luke")` would result in an alert box popping up that says "Hello, Luke".

CHAPTER 8

Macros

ClojureScript, like Clojure, uses *macros* to extend the syntax of the language. Fundamentally, a macro is just a function that manipulates data structures. What makes macros special is that they are invoked during the compilation process, to manipulate the data structures representing ClojureScript source code. Many of ClojureScript's core flow-control operators are implemented as macros, and you can write your own macros to extend the language.

Code as Data

Remember from Chapter 4 that all ClojureScript code is composed of data structures: lists, vectors, symbols, and so on. For example:

```
(println "Three plus four is" (+ 3 4))
```

We can read this expression as a list containing a symbol, a string, and another list. But to the ClojureScript compiler, that list represents a function call.

Macros allow you to manipulate the data structures in your code *before* they get to the compiler. This is very powerful: a macro can effectively rewrite code before it gets to the compiler.

Writing Macros

Macros are applied during the *compilation* process. They do not exist at runtime. Because the ClojureScript compiler is implemented in Clojure, ClojureScript macros must be *written* in Clojure, not ClojureScript. Fortunately, Clojure and ClojureScript are almost identical when it comes to manipulating data structures, so switching between the two languages is not difficult.

As an example, consider the when macro introduced in Chapter 4:

```
(when condition
  ;; ... expressions ...
  )

;; which expands to:
(if condition
  (do
    ;; ... expressions ...
    ))
```

The when macro is simply a way to avoid the extra do block when we want multiple expressions in an if expression. Usually this happens when the code inside the when macro is performing side effects.

To write a macro, first think about the expression you want to be able to *write* in your code. Second, think about what you want it to *become*. Finally, write a function that converts the first into the second. Here is a simple version of the when macro:

```
(defmacro when [condition & body]
  (list 'if condition
        (cons 'do body)))
```

Notice that a macro definition looks just like a function definition, but it starts with defmacro instead of defn. This function is variadic: it takes one argument called condition followed by any number of arguments that will be collected into the list called body. It then constructs a list starting with the symbol if, followed by the condition, followed by body with the do symbol inserted at the head.

Applying a macro is called *macroexpansion*, and it happens at the beginning of the ClojureScript compilation process. You can test it at the REPL with the macroexpand-1 function at the Clojure REPL. Remember, macros are written in Clojure, not Clojure-Script, so you must write and test them at the Clojure REPL.

```
user=> (macroexpand-1 '(when (even? 2) (println "2 is even")))
(if (even? 2) (do (println "2 is even")))
```

Notice that we are calling the macroexpand-1 function on a *quoted* form. We don't want to *evaluate* the when expression; we want to see what it will expand to during compilation. The macroexpand-1 function performs one round of macroexpansion. However, a macro can expand to code, which begins with another macro. To see the final result of all the expansions, you can call the macroexpand function, which keeps expanding macros until it reaches an expression that is not a macro.

There is also macroexpand-all, which recursively expands all the macros anywhere in an expression. It is available in the Clojure namespace clojure.walk. This macroexpand-all is not entirely correct because it doesn't recognize special forms such as let, but it is usually adequate for debugging macro expressions.

Syntax-Quote

Macros manipulate data structures that represent code. However, as the code they produce grows more complex, it becomes tedious to manually construct the data structures to represent it. To help, Clojure has the *syntax-quote* operator to construct "templates" for expansion. Syntax-quote is written using the backtick (`) symbol. It behaves like the normal single quote in that it prevents evaluation, but syntax-quote also allows values to be *unquoted*.

Here is a version of when written with syntax-quote:

```
(defmacro [condition & body]
  `(if ~condition (do ~@body)))
```

Notice that we don't have to do any manual construction, such as invoking list, as in the previous example. Instead, the syntax-quoted form looks similar to the form we ultimately want to produce. Within that form, we have unquoted the condition symbol by prefixing it with a tilde (~). We have used a variant of unquote called *unquote-splicing* on the body symbol. The unquote-splicing operator (~@) operates on lists by inserting the contents of the list at the expansion point, without the enclosing parentheses of the list itself. Unquote-splicing is like "unwrapping" a list before placing it in the expansion.

Auto-Gensyms

It is often necessary to create new symbols in the body of a macro, such as let bindings. To prevent these symbols from clashing with symbols already in use elsewhere around the code, Clojure's macros provide *auto-gensyms*, or automatically-generated symbols, guaranteed to have unique names. These symbols are generated by placing a hash sign (#) after the symbol name. Auto-gensyms are only available within a syntax-quoted expression.

For example, here is a macro that expands to some debugging code:

```
(defmacro debug [expr]
  `(let [result# ~expr]
     (println "Evaluating:" '~expr)
     (println "Result:" result#)
     result#))
```

In this example, the debug macro takes a single expression and uses it twice. To avoid evaluating expr more than once, it has to create an intermediate let binding. The result# symbol will expand to an auto-gensym, which is guaranteed to have a unique name that doesn't clash with any other symbols. Macroexpansion shows the result:

```
user=> (macroexpand-1 '(debug (println "hello")))
(clojure.core/let [result__6__auto__ (println "hello")]
  (clojure.core/println "Evaluating:" (quote (println "hello")))
  (clojure.core/println "Result:" result__6__auto__))
```

The debug macro also contains a clever trick: the "quote-unquote" in `'~expr`. This allows the expansion to print the literal code of `expr` without evaluating it.

Using Macros

Because macros are written in Clojure, they must be loaded differently in the ClojureScript compiler. To reference a macro from another namespace, add it to the `ns` declaration using the `:require-macros` form. For example:

```
(ns my-project.main
  (:require-macros [my-project.foo :as foo]))

(foo/my-macro)
```

This assumes that a *Clojure* source file is available on the classpath at `my_project/foo.clj` containing `defmacro foo`.

With the exception of the `ns` declaration, you generally do not need to think about whether you are calling a function or a macro in ClojureScript code. Many of the core flow-control structures of ClojureScript are implemented as macros (many of the core ClojureScript macros are actually the same as the core Clojure macros, invoked directly by the ClojureScript compiler!). The flow-control macros do not behave exactly like functions, because they can cause some of their arguments not to be evaluated. But well-written macros generally follow the behavior you expect: for example, ClojureScript's `and` and `or` macros are "short-circuiting" just like the Boolean operators in JavaScript.

When to Write Macros

The first answer to "When should I write a macro?" is usually "Don't!" Macros are the most powerful feature of a Lisp-like language, and the easiest to misuse. In general, you should always use functions and values as the primary units of abstraction in your code. Typically you only need macros in three cases:

1. To do things functions cannot do. For example, the `and` conditional operation cannot be written as a function, because it needs to prevent evaluation of some of its arguments. Macros can control when and how their arguments are evaluated.[1]

2. To add a layer of syntactic sugar. For example, the `when` macro doesn't do anything different from what you can already accomplish with `if` and `do`, but it makes the syntax shorter and easier to read.

---

1. Technically, you can prevent evaluation of function arguments by wrapping each argument in an anonymous function, but this is syntactically cumbersome.

3. To improve performance. Because macros are evaluated during compilation, they can potentially convert an expression into a more-efficient form before it reaches the compiler. The ClojureScript compiler uses macros internally to produce more efficient code, but you are unlikely to encounter this situation in everyday programming.

Summary

Macros are an extremely powerful language tool, so powerful that they are rarely needed in everyday programming. However, for advanced tasks, such as defining new control structures or embedding domain-specific languages, they can be invaluable. This chapter has barely scratched the surface of what macros can do. For more examples, refer to books about Clojure. For even deeper exploration of macros, look to books on Common Lisp, such as Paul Graham's classic *On Lisp* (*http://www.paulgraham.com/onlisp text.html*), available free online. Note that most other Lisps use the comma character instead of tilde for unquote.

CHAPTER 9

Development Process and Workflow

At the beginning of the book, we introduced Leiningen with *lein-cljsbuild* as an easy way to get started with ClojureScript. However, it is far from being the only way to work with ClojureScript.

This chapter will give a brief overview of some alternative means of installing Clojure-Script (including the cutting-edge development branch), as well as instructions on how to use the more low-level tools included with ClojureScript to compile manually or script your own personal workflow. It will also include some pointers to more advanced features of Leiningen that you may find useful for particular tasks.

Most importantly, perhaps, it also includes a discussion of the ClojureScript browser REPL, which you can use for interactive coding in a live browser environment.

Installing ClojureScript

Leiningen works by referencing the ClojureScript JAR file directly from a public Maven repository (via a local cache on your computer, of course). The Maven release, however, does not include some of the command-line tools and tests included in the source release.

In addition, the source release includes cutting-edge features from the master Git branch, whereas the Maven repository will only contain the latest milestone releases. For most production or educational work, the milestone releases are desirable, but bug fixes are often available much sooner on the master branch. If you're developing a Clo-jureScript library or tools for working with ClojureScript, you should consider testing your code on the master branch frequently for advance warning of any incompatibilities, so you can have them sorted out before the next milestone release.

There are two ways of obtaining the ClojureScript source code: checking out directly from Git, and downloading a zip or tar archive from GitHub.

Checking Out from Source Control

Start up a command line, and navigate to the directory where you would like to install ClojureScript. Then, just execute the following Git command to clone the repository:

```
git clone https://github.com/clojure/clojurescript.git
```

By default, Git will check out the most recent code from the master branch into a directory called `clojurescript`. If you want to run the bleeding-edge development version of ClojureScript, nothing else is required. However, you might wish to use a tagged milestone release, for greater reliability. (Although broken code is rarely checked in to master, it can happen on occasion).

To see a list of available tags, just use the `git tag` command. At the time of this writing, the most recent tag is `r1450`. To check out the tagged code, run a Git checkout on the tag. For example:

```
git checkout r1450
```

Your "clojurescript" directory will now contain the r1450 version of ClojureScript.

Downloading a Compressed Archive

GitHub provides the capability to download the repository as a zip or tar file, which does not require you to install the `git` program itself. The easiest place to do this is from the GitHub *tags* view, located here (*https://github.com/clojure/clojurescript/tags*). This page lists all the tagged versions of ClojureScript; each is a hyperlink to a zip file. Hovering over the link will also reveal a link to a tar archive. Click the most recent tag to download that version. If you wish to download the latest master branch, visit this page (*https://github.com/clojure/clojurescript/downloads*) and click "download as zip" or "download as tar.gz".

Extracting the downloaded file will create a directory that contains the entire ClojureScript repository, which is everything you need to get started using ClojureScript. You may wish to rename the directory to something simpler (such as "clojurescript"), instead of the default name, which includes the full repository name and commit hash ID.

Whether you installed via Git or archive, you should have ended up with a directory somewhere on your system containing the ClojureScript distribution. A common practice is to set up a `CLOJURESCRIPT_HOME` environment variable pointing to this directory, for convenience. The installation directory will be referred to as `CLOJURESCRIPT_HOME` throughout the rest of this chapter.

Installing Dependencies

Before you can use ClojureScript, you will need to download and install ClojureScript's dependencies.

For Unix-based systems (including OS X), ClojureScript provides a script that makes the process easy. Just navigate to the CLOJURESCRIPT_HOME directory you just set up, and run the bootstrap script:

```
./script/bootstrap
```

This will automatically download and install everything else ClojureScript needs to run.

Unfortunately there is no automatic bootstrap script for Windows users. Instead, you must install ClojureScript's dependencies yourself.[1]

These instructions may change over time as features are added to ClojureScript, so rather than committing them to print, you should look them up on the Windows installation wiki page on the ClojureScript GitHub site (*https://github.com/clojure/clojurescript/wiki/Windows-Setup*).

The Built-In Tools

Command-Line Compilation

ClojureScript includes a command-line tool for compiling *.cljs* files to *.js* files: the cljsc or cljsc.bat script (depending on platform) located in CLOJURESCRIPT_HOME/bin. It is a common practice to add CLOJURESCRIPT_HOME/bin to your system's executable PATH, so you can easily run cljsc from anywhere.

The command takes two arguments. The first is the path of either a single *.cljs* file or a directory containing *.cljs* files (in which case they will all be compiled together). The second argument is a string representation of the ClojureScript compiler options map, and should be enclosed in single quotes. Invoking cljsc looks something like this:

```
cljsc my/src/dir '{:optimizations :advanced, :output-to "out.js"}'
```

Note that you'll definitely want to specify an :output-to key in the compiler options; if you don't, the entire compiled output will be dumped to standard out, which in most cases is not what you want (although it can be useful, on occasion, as part of a longer scripted compilation chain).

---

1. At the time of this writing, the command-line ClojureScript tools have not been tested on the Cygwin Unix environment for Windows. We recommend either running a Linux virtual machine or following the Windows installation instructions.

Clojure REPL

If you just want to get started with a Clojure REPL, but with all the ClojureScript classes loaded on the classpath and ready to go, you can use the `script/repl` (or `script/repl.bat` for Windows) script in `CLOJURESCRIPT_HOME`. Launching it will start a basic Clojure REPL, but with everything you need to use ClojureScript already loaded into the classpath.

ClojureScript REPL

If all you want to do is run ClojureScript itself in a headless (nonbrowser) REPL, the fastest way to get started is to run the `script/repljs` script (`script/repljs.bat` for Windows), which launches straight into a ClojureScript REPL running in the headless Rhino JavaScript interpreter. You won't have access to any browser-specific features, but will be able to experiment freely with the language itself, as well as its standard libraries.

The Browser REPL

One of the main benefits of using a language from the Lisp family is the dynamic, highly interactive development workflow. However, since ClojureScript does not natively support the `eval` function, it requires the support of a Clojure runtime running the ClojureScript compiler to compile forms for execution in a REPL.

For local REPLs (such as the Rhino REPL), this is easy: the REPL just runs in the same JVM/Clojure process as the ClojureScript compiler and hands off forms for compilation. To achieve the same effect in the browser, however, requires that there be some sort of communication channel between the browser's JavaScript runtime environment, and the ClojureScript compiler running in a JVM.

Therefore, there are two parts to the ClojureScript browser REPL (often abbreviated *bREPL*), which operate in a client/server configuration. The bREPL *server* runs in the same JVM process as the ClojureScript compiler and exposes a REPL for developer interaction. The bREPL *client* runs in ClojureScript in the browser itself, and maintains a long-poll connection to the server so it can receive push messages (Figure 9-1).

Whenever you type a form in the bREPL, the server feeds it to the ClojureScript compiler and pushes the emitted JavaScript code to the client. There, it is evaluated in the browser's JavaScript context, where it may cause side effects that will be visible in the browser window. The return value of the expression is stringified (using the ClojureScript `pr-str` function) and sent back to the bREPL, where it is printed out as the expression's return value.

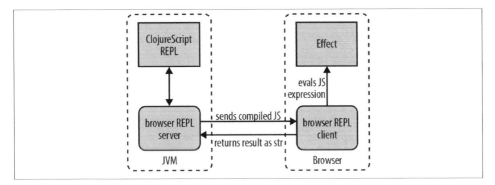

Figure 9-1. The ClojureScript Browser REPL

Setting Up the Browser REPL

Needless to say, this does require a bit of configuration—not only is it necessary to start the bREPL server, but you must also initiate the bREPL on the client side to establish the client/server connection.

Unfortunately, there is also one more requirement to use the browser REPL. Due to the restrictions browsers enforce to prevent cross-site scripting attacks, and the fact that the bREPL runs on localhost, the client page must *also* run on localhost. This means that, unlike the examples presented earlier in this book, you can't just create a static HTML page referencing your ClojureScript code and load it from a file: URL. Instead, you must serve the client page from an actual HTTP server running on localhost.

The most straightforward way to do this is to set up your Leiningen project to include a Ring application running on an embedded Jetty web server, and use Compojure to configure it to serve HTML files from the resources/public directory. Ring is a low-level HTTP web application library with wide adoption in the Clojure community. It is used as the foundation for most Clojure web applications. You can learn about it on its GitHub page (*http://bit.ly/QTxucf*). Compojure is a popular web routing library for Ring that makes it easy to configure web routes. Its page is here (*http://bit.ly/PP4gQU*).

Although any technique for serving resources from a localhost address will work, we will use Ring and Compojure since they are relatively easy to set up, and are by far the most popular ways to set up a Clojure web app.

Once you're set up to serve resources, all you need to do is start the Ring server at the beginning of your development session, and you can serve up the HTML files as you work on them just as you did when referencing the files statically.

Serving your HTML via Ring and Compojure

Modify your Leiningen project (or create a new one) so the `project.clj` includes Compojure and the Ring-Jetty adapter as dependencies. It should look something like the following:

```
(defproject brepl-hello "0.1.0-SNAPSHOT"
  :plugins [[lein-cljsbuild "0.2.7"]]
  :dependencies [[org.clojure/clojure "1.4.0"]
                 [org.clojure/clojurescript "0.0-1450"]
                 [compojure "1.1.0"]
                 [ring/ring-jetty-adapter "1.1.1"]]
  :source-paths ["src/clj"]
  :cljsbuild {
    :builds [{
        :source-path "src/cljs"
        :compiler {
          :output-to "resources/public/brepl-hello.js"
          :optimizations :whitespace
          :pretty-print true}}]})
```

Then, at a Clojure REPL, you can start a Ring server configured to serve resources from the `resources/public` directory on port 3000:

```
(use 'ring.adapter.jetty)
(use 'compojure.route)
(run-jetty (resources "/") {:port 3000 :join? false})
```

You can verify that the server is working by placing a file (for example, `test.html`) in `resources/public`, then hitting `http://localhost:3000/test.html` in your browser. You should see the contents of `test.html` served correctly.

If you don't want to start a Clojure REPL every time you start a server, you can use the *lein-ring* Leiningen plug-in, which allows you to add a server configuration directly to your `project.clj`, and start it by running `lein ring server` on the command line. See the *lein-ring* GitHub page (*https://github.com/weavejester/lein-ring/*) for configuration instructions.

Starting the bREPL server

Next, you must start the server component of the bREPL. This can be done from within a Clojure REPL (which you should already have open, after starting the Ring server). *lein-cljsbuild* also provides some convenience functions for starting a browser REPL server, which are covered later in "Additional lein-cljsbuild Features" (page 82).

From the Clojure REPL, run the following forms to start the browser REPL:

```
(require 'cljs.repl)
(require 'cljs.repl.browser)
(cljs.repl/repl (cljs.repl.browser/repl-env))
```

This will drop you into a ClojureScript REPL. Note that if you try to evaluate a form at this point, rather than returning a response, the REPL will simply hang. This is because we haven't yet configured the client side of the bREPL, which is required to actually evaluate the compiled JavaScript.

By default, the bREPL server runs on port 9000. If for some reason you need to run it on a different port, you can specify a :port key and value when creating a bREPL environment with the repl-env function:

```
(cljs.repl/repl (cljs.repl.browser/repl-env :port 8888))
```

Configuring the bREPL client

To connect to the bREPL server from within a browser, you must invoke the clojure.browser.repl/connect ClojureScript function in your client-side code. Typically, the easiest way to do this is to add an invocation to it as a top-level form in a ClojureScript namespace.

You can add it to an existing namespace, or create a new one as shown:

```
(ns brepl-hello
  (:require [clojure.browser.repl :as repl]))

(repl/connect "http://localhost:9000/repl")
```

If you changed the port on which you're running the bREPL server, you'll need to reflect that change in the URL passed to the connect function.

At the command line, compile the file with lein cljsbuild once. If your project.clj is configured like the example given above, this will emit a resources/public/brepl-hello.js file. Include it on an HTML page:

```
<!DOCTYPE html>
<html>
<head><title>ClojureScript bREPL Hello World</title></head>
<body>
    <script type="text/javascript" src="brepl-hello.js"></script>
</body>
</html>
```

If your Ring server and bREPL server are running, you can visit localhost:3000/brepl-hello.html in your browser, and upon loading, the bREPL client will establish a connection to the bREPL server and you can start evaluating forms. If you had already entered a form prior to starting the bREPL client, the REPL should have come "unstuck" as soon as you started the client and an execution environment became available.

To see an example of a live update to the HTML page, enter the following form at the browser REPL:

```
ClojureScript:cljs.user> (js/alert "Hello from bREPL!")
```

You should see a JavaScript alert box pop up from the web page. Congratulations! You now have a live REPL running against a real web page.

If you like, you can start your browser's debugging console and watch the bREPL send messages back and forth via AJAX requests as you type forms at the REPL.

Stability of the bREPL

Unfortunately, the browser REPL isn't as stable as it could be, although it is getting better. If it hangs, it's easy enough to restart, usually by refreshing the browser, but this can get annoying if you've already established state in the browser environment that you're working with.

A few tips to help you avoid bREPL crashes and lockups:

- Always start the bREPL server before loading the HTML page containing the bREPL client.

- Don't enter any expressions that return something that's not easily printable. These include infinite or very long sequences, very large data structures, and native browser objects that don't have a reasonable string representation.

- Don't enter any expressions that wipe the contents of the page (such as `document.write`). If you erase the page, it will also remove all scripts on the page and the bREPL client will disappear, causing the bREPL to hang.

- Try not to enter any expressions that will take longer than a few seconds to process. Some browsers will assume that the script has become unresponsive and will behave erratically, or prompt you to terminate it.

Additional lein-cljsbuild Features

lein-cljsbuild provides several features beyond the basic functionality we have covered so far.

Launching a Browser REPL

As you may have noticed while working through the browser REPL section above, starting up a Clojure REPL just to start a bREPL server can be annoying, and tedious if you have to do it often.

To alleviate this problem, *lein-cljsbuild* includes the `repl-listen` task, which will start a bREPL server and drop you into a ClojureScript REPL in a single step. Run it using this command:

```
lein trampoline cljsbuild repl-listen
```

(Recall that the `trampoline` task is necessary for Leiningen to receive interactive input.)

This command will start the bREPL server and a ClojureScript REPL in your current console. Note that you will still need to configure the bREPL client side as discussed above—the REPL started with `repl-listen` will not be functional until you've loaded a browser page with the client side code to establish the client-server connection.

Custom bREPL Launch Commands

lein-cljsbuild also offers a `repl-launch` command which, in addition to starting the bREPL server, also launches a browser for the bREPL client.

`repl-launch` does essentially the same thing as `repl-listen`, but also executes shell commands defined in the `:repl-launch-commands` key in the `:cljsbuild` configuration of `project.clj`. By specifying a vector representing a shell command that launches a browser, you can launch both the bREPL client and server with the same command. For example:

```
(defproject my-project "1.0.0-SNAPSHOT"
    ;; other leiningen configuration items
    :cljsbuild {
        ;; other configuration items & build configurations
        :repl-launch-commands {"firefox" ["firefox" "page.html"]}})
```

If you have the "firefox" binary on your system's PATH, you can run `lein trampoline cljsbuild repl-launch firefox`. The final parameter, `firefox`, will be looked up in the `:repl-launch-commands` map, and the associated command (`firefox page.html`) will be executed, launching Firefox and opening the specified page.

Of course, you are still responsible for ensuring that the page you specified (in this case, `page.html`) calls the `clojure.browser.repl/connect` function to launch the client side of the bREPL.

Hooking Into Default Leiningen Tasks

Normally, ClojureScript-specific build actions are triggered using the `lein cljsbuild` command, which pertains exclusively to ClojureScript code. However, for some projects, it's desirable to set up Leiningen to build everything at once.

To do this, it is necessary to add *hooks* to Leiningen's default tasks so that when you run `lein compile`, `lein clean`, or `lein jar`, the appropriate *lein-cljsbuild* plug-in task is also executed. *lein-cljsbuild* already includes these hooks; all you have to do is add them to the `:hooks` configuration key at the root of your `project.clj`:

```
(defproject my-project "1.0.0-SNAPSHOT"
    ;; ...
    :hooks [leiningen.cljsbuild])
```

Once you've added this line, invoking `lein compile` will kick off a ClojureScript compilation (the same as `lein cljsbuild once`). `lein clean` will also run `lein cljsbuild clean`, and `lein jar` will add ClojureScript source to the JAR if it's configured for that cljs build (see "Including ClojureScript in JAR Files" (page 85)).

Testing ClojureScript Code

There are a variety of ways to test ClojureScript code. *lein-cljsbuild* does not attempt to dictate a particular testing methodology or tools, but instead provides a generic hook for executing tests. By specifying a map of test configurations in a `:test-commands` key in the `:cljsbuild` configuration map, you can set up *lein-cljsbuild* to invoke any command-line sequence after compilation by invoking `lein cljsbuild test`.

For example, if you have ClojureScript tests that compile to a file called `resources/test/test.js`, you might wish to run the script in a headless browser such as PhantomJS (*http://phantomjs.org/*). At the command line, you would run them by executing `phantomjs resources/test/test.js`. To set up the same script to run within Leiningen, do something like this:

```
(defproject my-project "1.0.0-SNAPSHOT"
  ;; other leiningen configuration items
  :cljsbuild {
    ;; other configuration items & build configurations
    :test-commands {"unit" ["phantomjs" "resources/test/test.js"]}})
```

This will create a test configuration (named "unit"), so that when you run `lein cljsbuild test` it will first compile the ClojureScript, then execute the `phantomjs resources/test/test.js` shell command in a single step. Because the test command is just a system shell invocation, you can replace it with any command you like, making it flexible enough to use any testing runtime or framework you might choose. The downside is, of course, that you'll have to set up the test execution code yourself. But as long as you can run the tests from the command line, you can add them to the Leiningen test cycle using this technique.

The `:test-commands` configuration also supports capturing the `stdout` and `stderr` output streams from commands that it runs. To do this, add `:stdout` or `:stderr` key/value pairs after the command sequence:

```
(defproject my-project "1.0.0-SNAPSHOT"
  ;; ... other leiningen configuration items ...
  :cljsbuild {
    ;; ... other configuration items & build configurations ...
    :test-commands {"unit" ["phantomjs" "test.js" :stdout "test.out.txt"
                                                  :stderr "test.err.txt"]}})
```

With this configuration, output from the `phantomjs` process will be redirected to the `test.out.txt` and `test.out.err` files.

Note that you can also capture the output of `:repl-launch-commands` in the same way.

Including ClojureScript in JAR Files

If you're creating a ClojureScript library that you'd like to be available for other projects, it's a good idea to bundle it as a JAR file so that your clients can just add the JAR to their ClojureScript compiler classpath and start referencing your namespaces in their ClojureScript code.

By default, however, Leiningen does *not* include *.cljs files when creating a JAR file. To tell it to do so, you must first enable the *lein-cljsbuild* Leiningen hooks as described above.

Then, you must add the `:jar true` key to the ClojureScript build configurations you want included in the JAR file. When added, your `project.clj` looks something like this:

```
(defproject my-project "1.0.0-SNAPSHOT"
    ;; ... other leiningen configuration items ...
    :hooks [leiningen.cljsbuild]
    :cljsbuild {
        ;; ... other cljsbuild configuration items ...
        :builds [{:source-path "src/cljs"
                  ;; ... other build options ...
                  :jar true}]})
```

Once you've added these configuration items, you can build a JAR like you normally would in Leiningen, with `lein jar`. The emitted JAR file will contain all the *.cljs files specified in the build configuration, making them available on the classpath for any program that includes the JAR.

Compiling the Same Code as Clojure and ClojureScript

If you have code that is both valid Clojure and ClojureScript, *lein-cljsbuild* supports cross-compiling the code using its *crossovers* feature. Obviously, such code must consist only of the subset of Clojure that is also valid ClojureScript, and vice versa. It must not use any of the interop forms from either language, nor can it rely on any platform-specific features.

To use crossovers, specify a `:crossovers` key in the `:cljsbuild` configuration map. The value should be a vector of Clojure namespaces, which will then also be compiled as ClojureScript.

So, for example, if you have a namespace called `myapp.shared` that you want to be available as both Clojure and ClojureScript code, your `project.clj` might look something like this:

```
(defproject myapp "1.0.0-SNAPSHOT"
  ;; ... other leiningen configuration items ...
  :cljsbuild {
    ;; ... other cljsbuild configuration items & builds ...
    :crossovers [myapp.shared]]})
```

Under the hood, *lein-cljsbuild* implements this feature by literally copying the **.clj* files containing the specified namespaces, giving them a **.cljs* extension, and placing them in a interim directory, which is added to the ClojureScript source path. By default, it is *.crossover-cljs*. If you wish to use a different directory for this purpose, you may do so by specifying the desired path as the value of a `:crossover-path` key in the `:cljsbuild` configuration map. If you set `:crossover-jar` to true, the copied cross-over **.cljs* files will also be added when building JAR files (if *lein-cljsbuild* is configured to do so, as described in the previous section).

There is one additional caveat when using crossovers: code that contains macros. Because ClojureScript macros are actually written in Clojure, it isn't possible to simply copy Clojure files that contain macros to ClojureScript, and thus they won't work as crossover code as outlined above. *lein-cljsbuild* does provide some (arcane) tools for resolving this situation. Refer to *lein-cljsbuild*'s documentation on the feature here (*https://github.com/emezeske/lein-cljsbuild/blob/master/doc/CROSSOVERS.md*).

CHAPTER 10

Integration with Clojure

ClojureScript, as we have seen, is targeted primarily at web browsers. Although this makes it possible to design complete applications that run in a browser, it is even more powerful when combined with a web server running Clojure on the JVM. Clojure's literal data structures provide a rich data format for communication between a client and server, and with a little care you can even share code between the two languages.

AJAX

In spite of its original definition, Asynchronous JavaScript and XML, *AJAX* has become a catch-all term for rich client applications running in web browsers, communicating with a web server. The Google Closure Library provides the `goog.net.XhrIo` class to support asynchronous HTTP requests to a server across many different browser implementations.

Here is a simple example function that performs an HTTP POST request to a server:

```
(ns example
  (:require [goog.net.XhrIo :as xhr]))

(defn receiver [event]
  (let [response (.-target event)]
    (.write js/document (.getResponseText response))))

(defn post [url content]
  (xhr/send url receiver "POST" content))
```

The `goog.net.XhrIo/send` function takes a URL, a callback function, a method name, and an optional request body. When the server responds to the request, it will invoke the callback function on an object from which you can retrieve the status code, headers, and response body sent by the server.

The `goog.net.XhrIo` class and the associated `goog.net.XhrManager` class provide many more options for controlling HTTP server requests. Covering all of them is outside the scope of this book, but for more information you can consult the Google Closure Library[1] or Chapter 7 of Michael Bolin's *Closure: The Definitive Guide* (O'Reilly). In addition, some ClojureScript libraries are growing to support easier access to the HTTP features in the Google Closure Library; see Appendix A for details.

The Reader and Printer

Although they started with XML, many web browser applications now use *JSON* (JavaScript Object Notation) for communication between client and server. You can use JSON in ClojureScript as well: the Google Closure Library class `goog.json.Serializer` can serialize data to and from JSON, and there are several JSON libraries for Clojure.

However, JSON is a feeble data format when compared with Clojure's own literal syntax. It cannot distinguish between strings and keywords, and its maps (objects) only support strings as keys. Almost any application using JSON as a data format will eventually need to translate between native application data structures and their "lossy" JSON representations.

Clojure's data structures, on the other hand, are rich enough to represent almost any application domain, and they have a string representation that is just as compact as JSON. Furthermore, Clojure's literal data syntax is extensible, which we will explore later in this chapter.

Table 10-1 highlights the differences between JSON and Clojure data.

Table 10-1. JSON and Clojure data differences

Feature	JSON	Clojure
Numbers	Yes	Yes
Strings	Yes	Yes
Symbols	-	Yes
Keywords	-	Yes
Lists (Arrays)	Yes	Yes
Maps with string keys	Yes	Yes
Maps with arbitrary keys	-	Yes
Sets	-	Yes
Metadata	-	Yes
Extensibility	-	Yes

1. *http://bit.ly/TdqTtU*

Like any LISP-like language, both Clojure and ClojureScript have a *reader*, a function that transforms a stream of characters into data structures such as lists, maps, and sets. The ClojureScript compiler uses the same reader as the Clojure language runtime. The Clojure reader (invoked through the functions `read` and `read-string`) is implemented in the Java language, so it is not available to ClojureScript programs. But ClojureScript has its own reader, implemented in ClojureScript, which is designed to be fully compatible with the Clojure reader.

The ClojureScript reader is invoked through the function `cljs.reader/read-string`. As the name suggests, it takes a string argument and returns a single data structure read from that string:

```
(ns example (:require [cljs.reader :as reader]))

(reader/read-string "{:a 1 :b 2}")
;;=> {:a 1, :b 2}
```

The opposite of `read-string` is the built-in ClojureScript function `pr-str`, or "print to string," which takes a data structure and returns its string representation:

```
(pr-str {:language "ClojureScript"})
;;=> "{:language \"ClojureScript\"}"
```

Notice that `pr-str` automatically escapes special characters and places strings in double quotes, which the `print` and `println` functions do not:

```
(println {:language "ClojureScript"})
;; {:language ClojureScript}
;;=> nil
```

In general, the `print`, `println`, and `str` functions are used for human-readable output, whereas the `pr`, `prn`, and `pr-str` functions are used for machine-readable output.

Example Client-Server Application

Building a complete client-server application in Clojure and ClojureScript requires some knowledge of Clojure web libraries, which are outside the scope of this book. But the following example should give you an idea of how easy it is to communicate between the two languages.

This simple application will allow you to type Clojure expressions into a web form, evaluate them on the server, and display the result back in the web page.

Create a new project directory with the following `project.clj` file:

```
(defproject client-server "0.1.0-SNAPSHOT"
  :plugins [[lein-cljsbuild "0.2.7"]]
  :dependencies [[org.clojure/clojure "1.4.0"]
                 [org.clojure/clojurescript "0.0-1450"]
                 [domina "1.0.0"]
                 [compojure "1.1.0"]
```

```
                    [ring/ring-jetty-adapter "1.1.1"]]
    :source-paths ["src/clj"]
    :main client-server.server
    :cljsbuild {
      :builds [{
          :source-path "src/cljs"
          :compiler {
            :output-to "resources/public/client.js"
            :optimizations :whitespace
            :pretty-print true}}]})
```

Our application will use the Clojure libraries Ring[2] and Compojure[3] for the server side of the application, and the ClojureScript library Domina[4] for the client. Here is the server implementation, in the file src/clj/client_server/server.clj:

```
(ns client-server.server
  (:require [compojure.route :as route]
            [compojure.core :as compojure]
            [ring.util.response :as response]
            [ring.adapter.jetty :as jetty]))

(defn eval-clojure [request]
  (try
    (let [expr (read-string (slurp (:body request)))]
      (pr-str (eval expr)))
    (catch Throwable t
      (str "ERROR: " t))))

(compojure/defroutes app
  (compojure/POST "/eval" request (eval-clojure request))
  (compojure/GET "/" request
    (response/resource-response "public/index.html"))
  (route/resources "/"))

(defn -main []
  (prn "View the example at http://localhost:4000/")
  (jetty/run-jetty app {:join? true :port 4000}))
```

Next, the client side, at src/cljs/client_server/client.cljs:

```
(ns client-server.client
  (:require [goog.net.XhrIo :as xhr]
            [domina :as d]
            [domina.events :as events]))

(def result-id "eval-result")
(def expr-id "eval-expr")
```

2. *http://bit.ly/QiaNjY*

3. *http://bit.ly/QiaS7h*

4. *http://bit.ly/SQL6sZ*

```
(def button-id "eval-button")
(def url "/eval")

(defn receive-result [event]
  (d/set-text! (d/by-id result-id)
               (.getResponseText (.-target event)))))

(defn post-for-eval [expr-str]
  (xhr/send url receive-result "POST" expr-str))

(defn get-expr []
  (.-value (d/by-id expr-id)))

(defn ^:export main []
  (events/listen! (d/by-id button-id)
                  :click
                  (fn [event]
                    (post-for-eval (get-expr))
                    (events/stop-propagation event)
                    (events/prevent-default event))))
```

Finally, we need an HTML page to contain the application:

```
<html>
  <head>
    <title>ClojureScript Client-Server Example</title>
  </head>
  <body>
    <h1>ClojureScript Client-Server Example</h1>
    <form id="eval-form">
      <p><label for="eval-expr">
          Enter a Clojure expression to evaluate on the server:
        </label></p>
      <p><input id="eval-expr" name="eval-expr" type="text" size="70" /></p>
      <p><input id="eval-button" type="button" value="Eval" /></p>
    </form>
    <p>The result:</p>
    <pre id="eval-result">
    </pre>
    <script src="/client.js" language="javascript"></script>
    <script type="text/javascript" language="javascript">
        client_server.client.main()
    </script>
  </body>
</html>
```

This example is slightly different from most of the HTML in this book: the `<script>` tags are at the *bottom* of the file rather than in the `<head>`. This is necessary because the main function we defined in ClojureScript depends on the DOM elements for the form already being available. If the `script` tags were at the top of the file, there would be no reported errors but the event handler would never get attached to the Eval button and the application wouldn't work.

The Google Closure Library does not have an "on DOM ready" event as is commonly found in other JavaScript libraries. This was a deliberate choice for performance reasons: web browsers load JavaScript synchronously, blocking other rendering tasks. If you have a large `<script>` at the top of your HTML file, the browser will not render anything until that JavaScript has been downloaded, parsed, and evaluated. The Google Closure development team actually advocates placing `<script>` tags inline with HTML, just after the elements they depend on.[5] This approach yields maximum responsiveness but is complicated to implement. Placing `<script>` tags at the end of the document is an easier alternative that works consistently and is fast enough for most applications.

Once you have created the files for this application, you can compile it with `lein cljsbuild once` and run it with `lein run`. Visit `http://localhost:4000/` in your web browser and you should see an application page like Figure 10-1.

Figure 10-1. Screen shot of the demo application for this chapter

You can type an expression into the text box and click the Eval button to evaluate it. The result will appear below the form. Remember these expressions are being evaluated on the server, so they are in Clojure, not ClojureScript. You can see that by evaluating expressions that are only valid on the JVM, such as a BigInteger calculation:

```
(.pow (BigInteger. "2") 128)
```

Obviously this is a naïve implementation, and completely insecure. But it presents an idea of the possibilities of communicating between a client and server written in the same language, using the native data structures of that language as the data format.

---

5. This was discussed in a thread on the Google Closure Library mailing list (*http://bit.ly/SXAKth*).

You can even send ClojureScript expressions to the server, compile them with the ClojureScript compiler, and return JavaScript source code back to the browser for evaluation. ClojureScript's browser-attached REPL uses this technique, as do some experimental hybrid development environments.

 Session is an experimental browser-based REPL by Kovas Boguta; source code (*http://bit.ly/RUcLZ7*) and a demo video (*http://bit.ly/W1in7n*) are available. *Himera*, by Michael Fogus, presents the ClojureScript compiler as a web service; source code (*http://bit.ly/SVk1jP*) and a demo application (*http://bit.ly/RiBTG9*) are available.

Extending the Reader

Clojure 1.4.0 added extensibility to the reader in the form of *tagged literals*. A tagged literal is written as a hash (#) sign, followed by a symbol, followed by any other Clojure data structure. When the reader encounters a tagged literal, it looks up the tag in a table to find its associated reader function, then invokes that function to the following data structure as an argument. User code can define new tags and override the behavior of existing tags.

Clojure has a few built-in reader literals already, with more likely to come. For example, the #inst tag specifies an instant in time as a string in RFC 3339 format (*http://bit.ly/W1ib87*), like this:

```
#inst "2012-07-19T18:46:35.886-00:00"
```

The key feature of tagged literals is that they specify a precise *literal* representation but allow for different in-memory representations. The string after #inst must conform to RFC 3339, but Clojure on the JVM can parse it into one of several classes, such as java.util.Date or java.util.Calendar. The ClojureScript reader will parse the same instant literal into a JavaScript Date. When constructing a client-server application using both Clojure and ClojureScript, you no longer need to worry about converting dates to and from strings: you can print and read dates like any other native Clojure data structure.

User-Defined Tagged Literals

You can define your own reader literals as well. User-defined tags must be namespace-qualified symbols; all non-qualified symbols are reserved for future Clojure language extensions.

In Clojure on the JVM, the special file `data_readers.clj` contains a map from tag symbols to the fully-qualified names of functions that read them. You can also locally override the tagged literal functions by rebinding `*data-readers*`. In ClojureScript, you can add tagged literal functions with the `cljs.reader/register-tag-parser!` function, which takes a tag symbol and a function.

Keep in mind that tagged literal readers do *not* have access to the raw character stream. The Clojure(Script) reader will read in the characters that follow the tag, interpret them as a normal Clojure data structure, then invoke the tagged literal function *on the data structure*. The function should return a value, which *replaces* the tagged data structure in the final result.

Tagged literals are still a new feature in the Clojure language ecosystem, and support is evolving. Right now there is no well-defined API for printing tagged literals (in Clojure on the JVM, you can extend `print-method` to new types).

Sharing Code

As we have mentioned several times throughout this book, one of ClojureScript's strengths is that it is the same language as Clojure. As a result, you can share code between Clojure and ClojureScript. This is particularly powerful for client-server applications on the web. The *same code* can run on the client, compiled into JavaScript, as on the server, compiled into JVM bytecode.

As we have also stated repeatedly, shared code has to conform to a common subset of the features available in both environments. Code that does any of the following will *not* be shareable:

- Calls methods or classes of the host environment
- Interacts with host-environment resources such as the DOM
- Uses features that are only implemented in one host environment (such as Clojure's refs and vars, which ClojureScript does not support)
- Depends on behavior peculiar to the host environment (such as JavaScript's automatic conversion between strings and numbers)

Again, the point of ClojureScript is not to simulate Clojure and the JVM in a web browser. Clojure and ClojureScript are the same language, ported to different platforms. Clojure has been ported to other platforms, such as the .NET Common Language Runtime. Intrepid developers have even started modifying the ClojureScript compiler to emit code for other target languages including Scheme, Lua, and Objective C.

Techniques for sharing code between Clojure and ClojureScript are still evolving. In the simplest case, one can simply copy or symlink code in two directories. The *lein-cljsbuild* plug-in has a feature called *crossovers* to facilitate cross-language copying, as described in Chapter 9. If you want more precise control over how your code is compiled, you can invoke the ClojureScript compiler directly from Clojure. Future versions of Clojure and ClojureScript will likely include some kind of conditional evaluation or "feature expressions," making it possible to maintain a single source file that targets multiple host environments.

In any case, the possibilities of having a unified language across servers and web browsers are exciting. Consider some examples:

- The classic Model-View-Controller pattern, in which the Model can be mirrored on both client and server
- Unit-testing client and server code in the same process
- Debugging client code before running it in a browser

Summary

Being able to work in the same language and data model in both web browsers and web servers is the most compelling feature of ClojureScript. With a little care, most algorithmic or data-centric code can be made to work identically in Clojure and Clojure-Script. As both languages continue to develop, they will converge towards a common core, making it even easier to write code that targets both environments.

Libraries

Hopefully, this book has helped you to understand the basics of ClojureScript and how it works. But in order to build a real ClojureScript application, you'll need more than the basics. You'll need to manipulate the DOM. You'll need to send and receive AJAX requests and long-poll messages. You'll need to do drawing and visualizations.

Any one of these topics can be (and is) the subject of its own book, and unfortunately there isn't room to cover them all adequately here. However, you already have all the tools you need: with ClojureScript's capability to interoperate with JavaScript, you can access any JavaScript browser API, and consume any JavaScript library.

Additionally, despite the relative youth of ClojureScript, there is already a healthy crop of libraries designed not only to be compatible with ClojureScript, but to follow ClojureScript idioms and fit seamlessly into your application. Here, we will briefly introduce several of them to help give you an idea of the landscape.

ClojureScript's Standard Library

Lots of things you might want to do are actually already included in ClojureScript. There are many library namespaces available besides just `cljs.core`.

cljs.reader
> We covered the reader in Chapter 10. Unlike Clojure's reader, the ClojureScript reader lives in a separate namespace.

clojure.set
> Contains set manipulation functions such as `union`, `intersection`, `difference`, etc.

clojure.string
> Contains a variety of useful string manipulation functions, including `split`, `join`, and `replace`.

clojure.walk
> Contains tools for recursively walking and manipulating nested data structures in a functional style.

clojure.zip
> Contains an efficient implementation of *zippers*, a useful data structure for fully-functional yet performant tree navigation and manipulation.

Google Closure Library

Although the Google Closure library isn't itself written in ClojureScript, it is still extremely easy to use from ClojureScript. In fact, it's bundled with the ClojureScript distribution, and ClojureScript's standard library itself uses it. All you need to use it is to `:require` the namespace you want—it's already on your project's compile classpath.

The library itself is quite large. It contains over 50 namespaces, ranging from basic low-level functionality all the way up to elaborate UI widgets. Documentation can be found here (*http://closure-library.googlecode.com/svn/docs/index.html*).

For ClojureScript, some pieces of the library are more useful than others. Components written in a functional style (such as most of `string`, `math`, `dom`, and `crypt`) fit into any ClojureScript application seamlessly.

Others, like most of the UI code, are written in a very object-oriented style that, while completely usable from ClojureScript, are less convenient. These libraries will require a bit more work to fit into a ClojureScript program cleanly, but can provide powerful capabilities that would be extremely time-consuming to rewrite in pure ClojureScript.

Domina

Domina (*https://github.com/levand/domina*) is a DOM manipulation library for ClojureScript aiming to provide basic DOM manipulation capabilities in a convenient and idiomatic way. It is cross-browser, wrapping the DOM component of the Google Closure library.

It is loosely inspired by jQuery in that it supports easy querying to retrieve sets of nodes, and its operations usually accept and return node sets. The major difference from JQuery is that the concept of a "NodeSet" (called "DomContent" in Domina) is not a reified object, but a polymorphic abstraction over a variety of native concrete types including HTML NodeLists, individual nodes, arrays of nodes, XPath or CSS selections, etc.

In theory, this allows it to be more composable, allowing other libraries to supply new operations on DomContent, or create implementations of it against new concrete types.

Enfocus

Enfocus (*http://ckirkendall.github.com/enfocus-site/*) is another excellent DOM manipulation and templating library. It focuses on higher-level manipulations such as transformations, events, and animation effects, and is heavily influenced by the popular Enlive templating library for Clojure.

Enfocus is intended to be complimentary to Domina—in fact, Enfocus builds its high-level transformations on top of the lower-level features Domina provides.

Jayq

Jayq (*https://github.com/ibdknox/jayq*) is a thin but quite complete wrapper for the extremely popular JQuery library for JavaScript. It allows users to leverage JQuery's DOM manipulation capabilities, cross-browser compatibility, and large mindshare in ClojureScript.

If you are familiar and comfortable with JQuery, then Jayq is likely to be a good choice for you.

C2

C2 (*http://keminglabs.com/c2/*) is a powerful data visualization library for ClojureScript inspired by the excellent D3 JavaScript library. It provides mechanisms for making declarative mappings from your ClojureScript data to interactive, dynamic visualizations such as charts, graphs, and maps.

It supports a heavily data-driven approach, meaning that once a data binding is established between ClojureScript data structures and visual elements, the visual elements can watch the data and update automatically based on changes.

If you intend to do any charting, graphing, or other graphical data representation in ClojureScript, C2 is worth a very close look.

core.logic

Originally built for Clojure, core.logic (*https://github.com/clojure/core.logic/*) is an extremely powerful logic/relational/declarative programming system that now supports ClojureScript as well. It is based on *miniKanren*, a logic programming system for Scheme invented by Daniel Friedman, William Byrd, and Oleg Kiselyov and explained in the wonderful book *The Reasoned Schemer* (MIT Press).

Logic programming allows users to express a problem declaratively, letting the implementation worry about the actual steps required to compute a solution. For certain classes of problems, this approach can be extremely concise and elegant.

Although the learning curve for logic programming can be steep, exploring core.logic is well worth it not just for the practical benefit to your programs, but as an educational tool to help you think about software development itself in new ways.

About the Authors

Stuart Sierra and **Luke VanderHart** are Clojure/ClojureScript developers, members of Clojure/core, and the authors of *Practical Clojure* (Apress, 2010). Stuart lives in New York City. Luke lives in Maryland.

Have it your way.

Get even more for your money.

Join the O'Reilly Community, and register the O'Reilly books you own. It's free, and you'll get:

- $4.99 ebook upgrade offer
- 40% upgrade offer on O'Reilly print books
- Membership discounts on books and events
- Free lifetime updates to ebooks and videos
- Multiple ebook formats, DRM FREE
- Participation in the O'Reilly community
- Newsletters
- Account management
- 100% Satisfaction Guarantee

Signing up is easy:

1. **Go to: oreilly.com/go/register**
2. **Create an O'Reilly login.**
3. **Provide your address.**
4. **Register your books.**

Note: English-language books only

To order books online:
oreilly.com/store

For questions about products or an order:
orders@oreilly.com

To sign up to get topic-specific email announcements and/or news about upcoming books, conferences, special offers, and new technologies:
elists@oreilly.com

For technical questions about book content:
booktech@oreilly.com

To submit new book proposals to our editors:
proposals@oreilly.com

O'Reilly books are available in multiple DRM-free ebook formats. For more information:
oreilly.com/ebooks

O'REILLY®

Spreading the knowledge of innovators   oreilly.com

23999424R00064

Made in the USA
Lexington, KY
02 July 2013